THREE FIELDS

(A Brother. A Sister.)

By Anderson Burke & Richard (Dick) Bradley

The powerful story of two families
and the choices they made.

Three Fields (A Brother. A Sister.)

For information contact:

The Arc

of Florida

The Arc of Florida
2898 Mahan Dr #1
Tallahassee, FL 32308
http://www.arcflorida.org

ISBN: 979-8-9878708-0-8

Library of Congress: 2023933975

Published by: Creative Projects International Inc.
4001 Santa Barbara Blvd. Ste 404
Naples, FL 34104
info@creativeprojintl.com

Cover Photograph by: Helen Norman
Cover Design by: Dina Justice

TABLE OF CONTENTS

Introduction to the 2023 edition

In April of 2022 my friend and Executive Director of The Arc of the St Johns Kathy Jackson sent me an email stating that the new Chief Executive Officer of The Arc of Florida, Alan Abramowitz, would like to discuss a plan to reissue the 2012 book Three Fields (brothers). While Three Fields (brothers) sold out of the hardcopy we all felt the story of my brother Eddie Burke could have reached a wider audience. Many State of Florida legislators were given copies as was the governor, Rick Scott with the intention of helping the lawmakers decide to better fund programs that benefitted people like Eddie. Alan's arrival as CEO ten years later and his interest in reissuing the book gave all of us involved in the 2012 project the hope we could add significantly to the story line. Most exciting would be the inclusion of the Bradley family's contrasting story of daughter Kathy. I had mentioned the Bradleys in a few of paragraphs in the 2012 edition but now we have the opportunity to present a fuller view of Kathy's life courtesy of Dick Bradley's included narrative.

This book is both a history and a contemporary take on how our society deals with those of us born with significant physical and mental challenges. It is also the story of two families and how each coped with two very special children.

The new edition also brings more focus on The Arc and especially the amazing journey of Kathy Jackson. It has been a great honor to have spent time with the caretakers at The Arc. My one hope as you read Three Fields (A Brother. A Sister.) is to convey how dedicated the staff of The Arc is in making sure we as a society offer a safe and nurturing home for special people like Kathy Bradley and Eddie Burke.

While these events take place in Florida from the mid - 1950s until the second decade of the 21st Century this is not solely a Florida story. Families all over the United States and World live similar lives. It is important to ensure The Arc's dedication to the Kathys and Eddies of the world continues.

A note on sources: My Mother, Betty Burke, kept extensive journals and correspondence. It is these I quote from directly and in italics. With my Father, Herbert Burke, I recorded a series of interviews with him in 2011 and quote from these recordings. AB

PART ONE

Anderson Burke

Eddie Burke

In early November 1959, an overwhelming and permanent sadness surged unchecked into the small brick rental house. This palpable darkness entered through the front door settling everywhere, in each room, behind every curtain and door. This gloom struck the lights dim, even the broad rays of sunlight that escaped into the house were filtered and full of floating dust as if the sun had been covered by gray gauze. So heavy was this burden that for the next forty - six years it colored each heartbeat of the woman who felt most responsible for bringing it into her home.

As a seven year old, I could not understand what had happened. And only after the span of many years did I come to have a hint of the events of late Fall 1959.

Just a few weeks before, everything was different.

Then, before I woke and prepared for second grade, my father, Herbert, would leave the house on Bordeau Avenue in the newly built Jacksonville, Florida suburb of Arlingwood for the hospital and his new position as the junior partner in a medical practice. My mother, Betty, pregnant at thirty - one, was several months younger than my father. She had stopped teaching earlier in the year to care for my twenty - month old brother and me and prepare for the birth of her third child. When my father returned each evening, my mother would place his warmed dinner on the table. After he finished his meal, the family would spend time together watching the black and white TV or playing monopoly. My father, after a short time, would return to the Formica topped dining table and break open a medical text or a patient's history to study. My mother would play stride piano, in the style of her own mother, or she would read to me.

Even now, it is hard to imagine that time before, as everything seemed so normal, so safe. There was no fear. There was a warm home and food and loving parents, a younger brother and a baby on the way. Grandparents would visit several times a year. Cousins were nearby. Up and down Bordeau Avenue and across the city and across the country it was the same scene. Young families of war veterans were settling in, looking ahead to the promise of a new decade. Living in new suburbs, driving new cars, watching TV, climbing societal and professional ladders, birthing and rearing the group of children later known as baby boomers. We on Bordeau Avenue were deeply embedded in the promises of living in the greatest country and in the greatest time ever.

However, even in the months leading up to the birth of her third child, my mother had deeply ingrained reminders of an old dread. A fear that had been with her since childhood and one evident in 1959 by physical differences between her third pregnancy and her first two. This trepidation never left her at peace during her last pregnancy.

Forty - six years later I read from Betty's journal:

As a child, Mama and I would go to downtown Nashville on Saturdays and would end up on 5th Avenue at the 5&10 - cent stores. We would see an old, sad - looking lady with a mongoloid daughter looking at all of the wonderful merchandise in Kresses and Woolworth. I remember staring at them because Mama told me not to stare. When I was in college, I was again confronted with a mongoloid, a boy the son of the drug store owner. I became convinced I would have a mongoloid and after Herb and I were engaged I told him of this dread. He sort of laughed it off.

During the third pregnancy my parents discussed the old fear.

Herbert:

"I assumed that Betty was justified in being sad prior to the birth as I think all persons have good knowledge of what is going on," my father told me nearly fifty years later. He said my mother did not have the bulging abdomen so obvious in her previous pregnancies. She asked him why she did not have some sort of bulge.

"I told her the development can take place in a different position - not always balled up in a fetal position but sometimes stretched out. This implies breech delivery. Feet - out - first. I indicated to Betty her fears might be wrong. This was, however, more evidence to me that her feelings about Down syndrome were correct," he said.

"My feelings were neither medical or empathetic. I could not feel the way she felt. I told her she should not take the blame if the child has Down syndrome. We are both at blame genetically. I sided with Betty's feelings based on my history with patients...'What do you think is wrong?' I would ask a patient. Betty was certain she was carrying a Down syndrome child. She knew better than anyone else. I am also a direct cause of the baby...Without me there would be no baby. I tried to understand how she knew it was Down baby."

" 'It feels like it is,' she said."

"The baby in her did not move much. It was quite lethargic. I listened to her abdomen. Every now and then a foot could be felt under the stomach. Betty got sad on this basis. She knew it was Down syndrome but acknowledged it was our fault. I was hoping and praying it wasn't Down. I had lots of things to do. It wasn't on my mind all of the time. Nothing either of us could do anything about it but wait and give birth."

On a Saturday, 24 October 1959, my mother went into labor. The delivery was three weeks premature.

When the family reunited at home everything had changed. My mother spent time in her room behind a closed door. I could hear her crying. It seemed my father worked twenty - four hours a day. I could not understand what was happening. No one spoke. Lights in the house were kept low. Curtains were pulled tight against the daylight and perhaps curious neighbors. The small television was rarely on. Neither the record player nor the piano was played. Darkness defined the house on Bordeau Avenue. If my parents explained this change in our lives to me at the time, I have forgotten.

Early one evening I heard my mother's scream. The intensity of the scream overwhelmed me so immediately and completely that I still remember wiping tears away as I ran down the darkened hall to the living room. My mother stood next to the crib with her arms frozen, elbows out and her hands locked around her head. She was hunched over the crib as if she had been punched in the stomach. Her hair was uncombed and wild looking. The scream tapered off to a horrific rattle, leaving her mouth open, dark and terrifying. A man reached into the crib and pulled up the still baby. (For decades I assumed the man at the crib was my father.) He held the baby by the ankles upside down in one hand. The baby's arms and head flopped loosely. The man slapped the baby several times on the back. Each slap produced another horrible, frantic scream from my mother. He shook the baby trying to shock the lungs into working. Long moments passed. He thumped the infant's chest and shook the baby again. A spasm caused the infant's body to leap up. The baby wailed back to life.

This dark, surreal image is my earliest and for nearly five decades, the only memory I had of my new brother, Edward Morgan Burke.

The man who resuscitated the child, I later learned after reading my mother's journals, was her brother who stopped by each day after the birth to check on her. By the time I read her journal both he and my mother were dead.

As always, Floyd Whitlow stopped by after work. I was feeding Eddie his first solid food that Friday night when he became strangled and turned blue. Floyd Whitlow shook him by his feet to clear his throat. I was panicked so we called Margaret and she came over to keep the boys so that Floyd and I could go to the emergency room of St Vincent's Hospital to have Eddie checked. I was actually paranoid that someone would think I had, somehow, done this deliberately...

I can remember no more details about that evening in November 1959. Edward Morgan Burke then disappeared. With only a few unintended exceptions, the name of my youngest brother was rarely spoken in front of my middle brother or me. My middle brother for all appearances, within and outside the family became again, my youngest and only brother.

It was not until a month after the death of my mother forty - six years later and the discovery of her journals and files that I would see Edward Morgan Burke again.

* * *

On 9 March 1959, my mother turned thirty - one years old. She was in an exciting, transitional place in her life. While my father was completing his studies at Vanderbilt University Medical School, my mother taught elementary children in east Nashville near her childhood home. In addition, she taught long - term patients at Vanderbilt, General Hospital and at the Jewish Women's Society as a volunteer. Everything was about to change. She was preparing her young family for a move out of the cramped, run - down apartment assigned to my father at Nashville's VA Hospital. It had been our home for four years. The family was moving to the growing city of Jacksonville, Florida where a young cardiologist would be welcomed. As a third generation Floridian, my father was looking forward to a return to his home state. My mother's brother, Floyd, was stationed with the Air Force in Jacksonville. It was a coastal city bisected by the magnificent St. Johns River lying in the northeast corner of Florida along the Atlantic Ocean. With strong military bases, a thriving insurance business industry and plenty of new inexpensive housing developments, Jacksonville must have seemed like an exciting and ideal place to live. For my father, the move back to Florida was the next well - thought out step in his professional life.

Betty had two healthy boys and was married to a man with a promising medical career. All she wanted now was a daughter to make her life perfect.

Perhaps it was during the celebration of her birthday, but sometime in March of 1959 she became pregnant. The intent was to conceive a child and the timing was just right. Her ovaries had produced mature ovum, the female germ cell. The ovum moved from her ovaries into the fallopian tube to await a male germ cell.

Like sperm cells, each normal ovum contains twenty - three chromosomes. A chromosome is a thin strand of DNA responsible for carrying the genetic and hereditary information of the male and female cells forward. On each chromosome is anywhere between two hundred and fifty and two thousand genes. When combined to form a zygote, the resulting chromosome count will be forty - six. From that point on each cell division produces daughter cells containing forty - six chromosomes. This is the process that occurred in my mother's two previous pregnancies resulting in two medically normal boys.

However in March 1959, in that shoddy Nashville apartment, something caused a deviation resulting in superfluous chromosomal material on chromosome number twenty - one. This anomaly is referred to as Trisomy 21. No one yet knows why a bit of chromosome latches on to another strand of chromosome. But whatever the reason, the results are consistent. If brought to full term, the child will have Down syndrome. Recent studies have shown that in eighty - five to ninety - percent of cases, the extra copy of chromosome 21 is derived from the mother's ovum.

One or more of my father's sperm cells penetrated the thick wall of the waiting ovum. With a probable contribution of twenty - four chromosomes from my mother and twenty - three from my father, the zygote was formed with forty - seven chromosomes. Five to seven days after ovulation and fertilization, the zygote attached to the inner uterine wall. From that point on, each cell division produced cells with forty - seven chromosomes. As my middle brother lay in his crib and as I romped around the thin - walled apartment and as my father finished with his Vanderbilt studies and my mother taught ill children how to read and write, my developing sibling was marked irrevocably with the genetic disposition of Down syndrome.

Before leaving Nashville for Florida, my mother visited the family doctor one last time. When he had confirmed her pregnancy, she confided to him her fear of having a mongoloid child: *...the last time I took the boys to see the doctor, he had me promise to let him know what the new Burke "mongy" was....*

Betty's physician referred her to Dr. Stephen Lanier, a Vanderbilt Medical School classmate of his as the family's Jacksonville pediatrician.

My mother was three months pregnant when the family packed everything into a Chevrolet sedan and headed the six hundred miles south to a bright future in Jacksonville.

Even if Dr. Lanier had known she was carrying a Down syndrome child, nothing short of an abortion could have been done to change the outcome. There was, nor is there today, any medical treatment to remove or alter the extra chromosomal material from chromosome 21. Amniocentesis, the drawing of the amniotic fluid surrounding the fetus and studying it for chromosomal disorders, was used in the 1950s for limited diagnosis of blood diseases and to determine the sex of the fetus. It was not until 1968, that amniocentesis was used to determine if a fetus had Down syndrome. It was in the very year of Eddie's conception and birth that a French physician, Jerome Lejune, positively identified the chromosomal anomaly of Trisomy 21 as the cause for Down syndrome. Until 1959, scientists were unsure what caused Down syndrome.

In the delivery room, attentive medical staff, including my father, would have spotted certain characteristics in the prematurely born boy such as a lower than normal birth weight, low muscle tone, a flattened face, small ears with perhaps a fold of skin over each ear top, an upward slant of the eyes, an easily identifiable and distinct line across the palm and widely spaced first toes.

Herbert:

"I was scrubbed up as an observer. We were looking for any signs of Down syndrome in the delivery room. It was a headfirst birth. I stared at him as doctor wiped him off. He was not crying. The staff put silver nitrate in the eyes to kill any bacterial agent. They were cleaning him and I recognized he was not crying. Also he did not cry when tapped on his back. They then put a suction in his mouth to see if something was preventing crying. He was breathing so he was clear. I was looking to see if he had any signs of Down. I was looking for any variations from a perfectly normal birth.

"All of the nurses knew of Betty's fears. Her OB/GYN knew it.

"A nurse put him on the examining table. He was breathing OK. He was alive. His left arm was out and his palm was facing up. I grabbed his hand looking for a simian line. It was there, very distinct, very deep. I looked at the length of his fingers particularity the little one and noted that it was foreshortened and had a slight inward curvation, another sign of Down syndrome. I was trying to accumulate enough signs to know if he had Down. I noticed his ears were more rounded than oblong and they appeared smaller than the usual infant's at birth. The nurse performed the test for the Moro reflex."

To test for the Moro reflex, Eddie would have been placed on his back. The nurse would have supported his head in one hand, raising it before allowing it to fall backwards slightly. A healthy newborn will spread arms out working fingers and thumbs to grab onto something for support. Absence of this startle reflex can indicate severe brain damage.

Herbert:

"He did not have a Moro reflex. No response...The hope that it would not be Down syndrome was being eroded. With every sign,

I found a characteristic of Down. I knew he had an abnormal nervous system. I saw him lying on the table with not much arm or leg movement. I knew that if he proved not to be Down after all of the data was made, he would have some nervous system deficiencies. My knowledge of the syndrome and my hope that it wasn't Down ran in a conflicting way. It is possible to believe something so much it can appear to be there.

"The nurses were not saying anything. They weren't looking at Eddie the same way I was.

"Before they took Betty away, Dr. Lanier turned to me and said, 'what do you think, Herb?' I said, 'It seems likely that he has Down syndrome.' Lanier indicated he thought he had Down.

"Betty had tri - lane anesthesia. A gas. She could control the amount of gas. She was not out of it. She did not say anything or cry. She knew it was a boy. 'Can I see him now?'

"She saw the baby and I don't remember her crying or saying, 'I knew it' or 'I told you so.'

"After the birth, I went to the room with her but don't think we talked a lot. Within a day or two we all talked about Eddie having Down syndrome. However, the diagnosis was really made five minutes after he was born."

Once the more obvious signs of Down syndrome were spotted, there would have been a different atmosphere in the delivery room. The happiness normally associated with the arrival of a newborn would have been tempered. My mother had a different memory from my father's on the events that day in the delivery room and the next day while still in the hospital.

I went into labor about three weeks early on October 24, 1959 and called Herb at the office. Herb said the office was full of patients and he simply could not get away. Margaret came to keep the boys. I drove to the hospital. Herb came over after office hours and was in the delivery room with me. Edward Morgan Burke was born. I didn't see him until the next morning. The nurse handed him to me and said, "I've got to take him back for Dr. Lanier to examine.

The morning of 25 October 1959 my mother was alone in her hospital room. When she was handed the wrapped bundle, she peered into the face of her baby for, as she states in her journal, the first time. She was then confronted with her long held, deep fear.

The minute I looked at Eddie's face, I asked the nurse to please go get Dr. Lanier and I started crying. He was a mongoloid. Dr. Lanier was in shock. He kept saying that my dread and our conversations might have something to do with the fact he, too, thought Eddie was a Down syndrome child. The next few days in the hospital were a nightmarish blur. I was crushed that Herb had not been the one to tell me or that he wasn't present when I saw the baby.

In retrospect, I realize this baby was far less active; my reason for thinking it was a girl. I attempted to nurse him for a day or two but finally decided I didn't want to go through the frustration of trying to nurse Eddie.

My parents were handed a four - inch by two and a half - inch card from the hospital. Printed across the top of the card in light blue, now faded gray, are two angelic baby boys holding a garland of roses interspersed with hearts. Below the smiling figures written in blue ink are the dry statistics of Eddie's birth. The infant weighed five pounds and ten ounces. His recorded length was 18.5 inches. The mother was listed in room 333.

***

In 1866, an English physician, John Langdon Down published a paper defining the physical characteristics of such a child. He believed the flat face, small nose, eye shape and learning disabilities was a reversion to a primitive human type. The asiatic appearance of the eyes and face led Down to use the term, *mongolian idiocy* to describe such cases. For more than one hundred years the word, *mongoloid,* was used by scientists and lay people to describe people afflicted with the syndrome. In the 1960s at the request of the Mongolian People's Republic, *mongolism,* as a medical term, was officially declared archaic by the World Health

Organization. As a nod to Dr. J. L. Down, use of the more benign name, Down syndrome was encouraged.

Mongol, and its derivations and descriptives for someone with Down syndrome joined previous scientific and medical terms such as *idiot, cretin, fool, imbecile* and *retard* on the junk pile of words abused in the schoolyards, churches and homes in the United States.

***

Immediately after Eddie's birth, my father broke the news to my mother's brother, Floyd Whitlow who was waiting at the hospital for the birth of his new niece or nephew. No one wanted to tell my mother the news that night. Her premonition of giving birth to a Down syndrome child was well known.

The next few days in the hospital were a nightmare. I cried constantly and when I walked down to look at the babies, had to return to my room to cry again. Dr. Lanier told me they would send off Eddie's handprint to be tested in Atlanta for "tri - dent radius", a positive sign of Down syndrome. Dr. Lanier was the one person who seemed caring and I remember one day while still at the hospital, I asked should I keep the baby at home. He told me a story of the farmer who had three fields; two were fertile and the crops were good. One was infertile and could grow nothing on it. He said the farmer could neglect the one poor field and concentrate his efforts on the two good ones or he could spend his time on the bad one and neglect the two good ones.

Herbert:

"Lanier said, 'Herb, you have charged me with taking care of Edward and I accept that responsibility. You are to take him home, love him, do the normal things with him and we are going to confirm the diagnosis.' "

On 2 November 1959, an announcement of the birth appeared in the Florida Times - Union. Three months later, another birth announcement was posted in the Presbyterian Tidings, a pamphlet produced by the church the family attended. Neither announcement mentioned the dire condition Eddie nor the family was in.

***The next few** weeks were simply a blur. We had decided not to tell our families until we were sure of the diagnosis so I was trying to "keep up" on the phone conversations and letters to families and friends. I lost weight, couldn't sleep, cried most of the time, yet tried to keep life as normal as possible for the children. Waiting for the handprint result was agonizing.*

The prints of Eddie's palms, sent to an Atlanta laboratory, would have been examined for at least two markers of Down syndrome: a high number of ulna loop dermatoglyphics, that is the ridge configurations on palms, fingertips and on the soles of our feet and the presence of a "simian" crease running across the middle of the palm.

The ulna loop patterns are so named as the loop in the ridges start out on the little finger side of each hand, also the side of the hand closest to the ulna bone of forearms. A large number of ulna loops can be indicative of Down syndrome. The "simian" ridge as it was called at the time of Eddie's birth is found in approximately 65 - 70% of Down syndrome individuals. Now referred to as a single palmar crease to disassociate it with our primate cousins, the distinctive crease forms at about thirteen weeks and is a result of the three normal creases joining together to form one.

Dr. Lanier and my father knew from their medical perspective that Eddie had Down syndrome. My mother knew as well. Waiting for negative test results from Atlanta was an against all odds hope they all had.

I had an appointment with Dr. Lanier for the baby's four - week check up on a Friday. Herb had planned to go out of town for the weekend and I guess I resented the fact he had that planned for the day I was taking Eddie to Dr. Lanier. The check up proved what I knew. The baby had not gained weight and Dr. Lanier, with all kindness and seeming understanding, told me the baby was, indeed, mongoloid. Again we discussed whether to institutionalize him or not and decided the best thing in our case was to do so. Dr. Lanier was going to put the steps in motion as far as finding a place in Jacksonville to place Eddie as soon as possible. I remember driving home, crying the whole way.

My father's memory of the first four weeks of Eddie's life differ from my mother's journal entries. For me it is not important or necessary if one parent's memory is more accurate than the other. Both are equally valid. It was a time of high stress and grief, tempered by a nearly fifty - year gap from this period and now and extreme tensions existing at the time.

Herbert:

"They did the tests. Called us in and gave us the results...'We have the confirmation of severe Down syndrome.' The idea Eddie would be able to function at an acceptable range because of the severity would be very unlikely. Next we had to decide what would be Eddie's best future. We decided it would be as a ward of the State."

I asked my father if he recalled any family members or friends offering condolences or comments.

"None of that happened. I don't remember anybody visiting with us. I don't know why. If your mother felt that she was being neglected by the family in any way she did not express it to me. She was depressed enough over the whole situation. Nothing else could have made it any worse.

"I remember Lanier saying Eddie would have a better chance in life and happiness in life if he were in circumstances that offered him the most for survival. We did not say 'we want to keep him here and take care of him.' I did not know what was best for him. He said 'it would be better for your children and for Eddie and for everybody in your household in the long run to have him become a ward of the State.'

Dr. Lanier mailed two letters on 1 December 1959. One was to Mr. Joe Lorimer of the Juvenile Court of Duval County requesting a "very early admission" to the Sunland Training Center in Gainesville, Florida. To justify his request, Dr. Lanier added, "Mrs.

Burke has had a morbid fear of delivering a Mongoloid child since before the delivery of each of her other two normal children. She also had this same fear before this one, and now that he has turned out to be a true mongoloid, it is producing a great deal of tension in the house and a great psychological disturbance in the family. For this reason and for the effect this baby will have on his older brother (sic), I am asking to please expedite his admission as quickly as possible."

The second letter was to a judge, perhaps an acquaintance of the doctor's, asking assistance in getting Eddie placed "as soon as possible." For the birth of the mongoloid child "has produced a great deal of tension in the home and certain pressures have developed that are quite strong and for the safety of the home and the integrity of the persons involved, I am urging that Edward Morgan Burke be placed in Sunland Training Center...If you can in any way help us, this would be greatly appreciated."

Three days later, R.C. Philips, Superintendent of Sunland Training Center at Gainesville responded that the application for Eddie's admission was received and placed on an active waiting list. But, Mr. Phillips responding to Dr. Lanier's description of my mother's fear and resultant emotional shock, warned, "We cannot offer hope of early admission of this child, due to our long waiting list and limited facilities. Our average waiting period is from eighteen to twenty - four months."

Herbert:

"There was a period of time from when...We kept him at the house. He did not require any special type of care. No one had to come in and help your mother take care of him."

Several weeks later, Herb and I drove to a home in Riverside to give Eddie to a foster home, one which "specialized" in keeping babies until they could be placed. I honestly thought I was going to die when we were driving home and the few weeks before Christmas I was simply going through the motions.

Herbert:

"Over on Cherry Street along the river, I remember a big old oak tree and the lady that took care of Eddie. I don't remember how old he was when he was there. It was like he was waiting to go somewhere. I don't remember how long he stayed at Cherry Street. I went over there several times and talked with the lady. She was a nurse."

Because Mama was coming down for Christmas, we had to tell her but didn't tell the Burkes (Herbert's parents) *until after Christmas. Somehow, I wanted to keep from spoiling everyone's holiday.*

Herbert:

"The thing that I remember the most was the reaction of your mother. She did not want him to go to Sunland or anyplace. But she knew he had to go and it would be better for him. But she did not like it. She was expressing the very thing people do when they are departing from someplace. Intellectually, she gave him up. Emotionally, she didn't. So it was that typical, classic conflict.

"I do not know when he was declared an official ward of the State. I don't remember anybody coming over and interviewing us. I probably repressed all of that. It was a successful repression. I always felt it was best for him and best for the family that he be around teachers who could help him more than we could...Your mother developed that attitude too. It had to be. She never thought it was better for him to stay at home. It was better *for her* that he stayed at home. When that was pointed out to her, then conflict came into the situation."

Herb simply backed off from the baby. Period. Against his will and advice, I visited Eddie once a week. I would take him to Dr. Lanier's for check ups and shots. Dr. Lanier prescribed some medication to enable Eddie to gain weight. He had pneumonia during the next year and was put in Baptist Hospital for a few days. Still, Herb and I could not talk about him at all. I suppose we were handling it as best we could in our own way but I really needed to talk about him. I was checking out from the library any book I could find on the problem. I went to Dr. Harvin at our church and he advised me to pray about it and mentioned a fellow pastor at Riverside Presbyterian Church who had a mongoloid. I made an appointment with him. He was a Godsend and encouraged me to accept the fact we had done the right thing in institutionalizing Eddie.

In 1956, the Mental Health Materials Center, Inc. of New York City published a sixteen - page pamphlet titled, "Deciding what's best for your retarded child." The author was Katherine G. Ecob, a well - known and respected authority on what was referred to at the time as "mental retardation." Ecob wrote that the family has three basic considerations when dealing with a retarded child: The welfare of the retarded child, the welfare of the family and the welfare of society. Ecob recognized that keeping a retarded child in the home "gives more affection and individual attention than any institution can supply…the child is brought up in the world of reality." Ecob understood however that keeping a child in the home is not always the best option: "The objective is to make the child's life happy, and as useful as the conditions permits while keeping the overall welfare of the family intact… A retarded child is an unusual responsibility, and requires many family adjustments. How much he will disturb the family life depends on many factors…If such conditions exist and are not likely to improve, then institutional care is indicated for the greatest good of the greatest number... The so called Mongolian type is often singled out as being in need of institutional care…"

The remaining ten pages of the pamphlet discuss the benefits institutions provide for a mentally retarded child, especially one considered severely retarded.

With this pamphlet, and many more written in the era predating Eddie's birth, the general consensus of the 1950s seems to recommend institutionalizing severely mentally retarded children as early as possible in order to offer the most help for the child and to protect the integrity of the family. "The mother," the pamphlet advises, "who has most of the care of the child, may become incapacitated. Other children may suffer chronic illness. The father, who supports the family, may lose his job so that the mother has to work. The death of either parent will alter the whole picture. Such serious changes often indicate institutional care."

Herbert:

"I remember the ideas and results of our discussions. We felt Sunland policies could do more for him than we could do. It was State supported and provided a haven for people who might need some safety in growing up."

On 21 September 1960, nine months after Dr. Lanier's letter requesting placement at Sunland, Mr. Philips sent a letter to the Juvenile Court advising that Sunland was in the "position to accept Edward Morgan Burke as a patient at Sunland Training Center...We ask that this applicant be delivered to us during the week of October 3 between the hours of 9 and 11 a.m. and 2 and 4 p.m. Monday thru Friday. We cannot hold a place open longer than the last day of the period mentioned above and if the applicant is not brought to us within that time, we will be forced to consider our acceptance cancelled."

Herbert:

"I do not know who exactly made the arrangements. I know I didn't. I didn't call anybody in the State. Who took him to Sunland? I don't know. Your mother may have taken him over there."

We were notified that Sunland Training Center in Gainesville had an opening and we were to bring Eddie on a certain day. Herb did not want to take off work that day so Margaret Whitlow drove my car. I held the baby. Eddie had grown but could not sit up or hold his head up.

Edward Morgan Burke was eleven months and 20 days old when he was picked up at the nurse's Cherry Street home by my mother and her sister - in - law.

My mother with the baby on her lap and her sister - in - law driving would have traveled west out of Jacksonville on Highway 90 some miles before turning south on Highway 301. Passing through hardwood and pine stands, overgrown ditches, small farms, shotgun shacks with truck patches, family owned motels not yet affected by coming interstate roads, produce and citrus stands, groves of pecan trees, lumber mills, and the speed trap towns of Lawtey, Starke and Waldo before turning west on Highway 24 toward Gainesville. Twenty minutes later, they would have come upon Sunland, a two - hour drive from Jacksonville. It must have been a dreadful drive for both women.

Sunland occupied 1,300 acres of hard packed, sand hill land on the southeast side of the Waldo Road. Tall long leaf pines, moss covered oaks and planted azalea bushes covered the grounds. On 4 October 1960 Eddie was almost one year old. After leaving the hospital where he was born Sunland would be his third home. Upon arrival there would have been no bright welcoming display of flowers from the azalea bushes to greet the travelers. If that Tuesday had been a sunny day, large patches of shade offered respite to the visitor and resident. Islands of fallen pine needles turned orange and brown floated lightly on cropped green grasses offered a soft place for staff and residents and their families to sit and picnic. Sunland was designed as a peaceful setting, designed as a beautiful and reassuring place for a parent to leave a child. If it weren't for the widely spaced brick and wood buildings housing and serving nearly two thousand children, Sunland could have been an inviting public park. If the general attractiveness of Sunland made an impression on my mother, she left no record of it. I would guess the grief of permanently giving up her child to the State of Florida blotted out any positive aspects of the facility.

The one lane entrance road to Sunland passed by a guard shack before winding left to the Administration Building. Betty would have held her baby tighter looking down at the unfocused eyes while Margaret notified someone in administration the Burke child, Edward Morgan, was here as scheduled. She would have been instructed to drive the child to the hospital where he would have been officially checked in. After leaving Eddie at Sunland, Betty and Margaret would have, with little conversation, retraced their journey of that morning back to Jacksonville and to a new level of existence Betty had long feared.

***

In the late 1800s, the idea of creating institutions for the mentally retarded with a more home - like feel spread around the country. The State of New Jersey adopted the cottage plan concept in 1892. The Farmington State Hospital in Missouri followed in 1903. Even the labeling shifted from terms like "asylum for the insane" to a much more friendly reference, "State hospital". In January 1909, President Teddy Roosevelt hosted a White House Conference on the Care of Dependent Children. One goal of this conference was to "...Emphasize the urgent need to respond more effectively to children who were poor, orphaned, abandoned, abused or neglected." Over two hundred experts on childhood problems attended the event. What emerged from the conference was the recognition that, "it was appropriate to care for mentally retarded...in specialized institutions," and the "recommendation was that institutions should be on the cottage plan with small units, as far as possible."

Following the trend established in Missouri, New Jersey and suggested by Roosevelt's conference, the State of Florida, in 1915, appointed a commission to investigate "the need of a state institution for the care of the indigent, epileptic and the feeble minded."

After four years of study, the commission returned to the Legislature and recommended a state institution for the "unfortunates." Acting quickly, the State, in 1921, opened the Florida Farm Colony for the Epileptic and Feeble Minded on 3,000 acres of land donated by Alachua County (Gainesville). By 1923, more buildings had been added to the original three, housing a total of two hundred and forty two people. By 1930, additional buildings popped up on the grounds providing administration and cottage housing for well over four hundred persons. By the mid to late - 1950s, the name, Florida Farm Colony, had been replaced by the more progressive and user friendly name, Sunland Training Center. Management of Sunland was handed over to the State of Florida's Division of Child Training Schools.

At the time Eddie was admitted to Sunland, the architectural and engineering firm of Connell, Pierce, Garland and Friedman was preparing a seventy - three page booklet for the State of Florida entitled "Sunland Training Centers for the Mentally Retarded in Florida."

Released in the summer of 1961, "Sunland Training Centers for the Mentally Retarded in Florida" addresses what parents would want for their retarded children: The parents "would make every effort within their means to create an environment which would allow the child to get the most out of life himself. This would include above all sympathetic loving care. It would include happy, healthful surroundings and wholesome physical activity to the extent possible. It would include learning - first, personal care; then, usable skills to the limit of the child's ability. Finally, it would include religious training and rewarded service to the limit of the child's ability.

"Few, if any, homes are equipped to supply an environment which reasonably fulfills the above requirements for their mentally retarded children." The report addresses what would be a parent's ongoing nightmare…what would happen to their child, if raised at home, when the parents die? "…The child finds himself completely incapable of facing the outside world when the mother and father die. This may be 10 - 15 or 20 years before the expiration of the child…an adult child."

And for parents like my own who searched for justification and emotional backup, page two of the booklet offers, "…when it is found by the family and competent authority that it is the best for the mentally retarded child to be away from his family (best for the child, best for the family or best for both), there is no apparent civilized humane course but to build and maintain institutions sympathetic to the needs (all the needs) of the mentally retarded child."

Once my mother handed over her youngest child to the State, Eddie would have spent some time in the facility's hospital being evaluated for placement. Due to his young age and estimated degree of retardation, Eddie would have been placed in an open bay ward in a cottage for infants. His immediate world would have been an enclosed crib watched over by twenty - four hour supervision. The Connell study reported over nineteen hundred children being attended to at Sunland by a staff of 1,114. If a child was physically capable of eating in one of the two main dining rooms, he or she joined other children for meals. Those too young like Eddie or those incapable of walking would have been served food from heated food carts brought to their crib or cottage room.

***

For several years *without Herb's knowledge, I drove to Gainesville to see Eddie at least once a month but days before and after the trip, I would be terribly depressed and the trip back was always terribly emotional for me…When he was four or five and finally crawling, I took him for a drive around the grounds of Sunland one day. As I was carrying him back into his cottage, I was spat upon by him repeatedly and I honestly wish he had died at birth or I had miscarried; anything but what Herb and I let his condition do to us. I really had murderous thoughts and that day driving home, I thought about suicide very briefly. I finally realized that my visiting him was a way of appeasing my guilt or trying to and that my lows involved with visiting were of no benefit to anyone, especially me. So, sometime in the mid - sixties, I backed away from these visits.*

In a 1990 letter to an administrator at Sunland, my mother reiterated what she had written in her journal: *Even after he moved to Gainesville, I sneaked to see him. The last time I drove over to Gainesville, I put Eddie in the car and drove him around the grounds. At some point, I considered kidnapping him and going off - just the two of us. That day driving home, I made the decision to heed the advice of a very old but well respected nurse (she had once been the president of the national ANA). She had written upon hearing about Eddie's condition to think of a farmer with three fields, two of which were fertile - one sterile. He could spend all his time on the sterile one, thus losing the other two or vice versa. I decided that day to spend my time and energy and emotional well being on my two good fields. I also realized that I was simply beating myself to death visiting Eddie…I never returned.*

Whether she had received a letter from a nurse with the same three fields analogy given to her by her physician or simply forgotten the source of the advice I will never know.

In July of 1961, the State of Florida acquired the recently closed Graham Air Force base, located outside the panhandle town of Marianna. In January 1963 Sunland Marianna opened at the former military base as part of an overall plan to serve the growing population with special needs of the State. Sunland Marianna was to absorb severely retarded individuals from Sunland Gainesville. Still considered housing and maintenance facilities, there was little thought of rehabilitation or training of the patients.

***

As earlier described, Eddie disappeared from my expanding world in 1960. I do not remember if I was too frightened to ask about the baby or whether I thought this was a normal event all families lived through. What could I have been thinking at seven years? Life seemed to move along. School, sports, cub scouts, home. Those frightening moments at Eddie's crib became like a scene from a movie. I wasn't sure if it was real.

I had two parents, a younger brother at home, extended family, friends and school. However, an irreparable crack had formed in my parent's marriage. At some point, my mother ceased loving my father. My father sensing this change began to spend most of the day at the office or hospital. I do not remember his being home for many meals and attributed his absence to the demands of his medical practice.

On rare occasions, I heard the name, Eddie. Perhaps it had been a grandmother asking about him in a moment when she thought the children were out of the room. Or a neighbor my mother had confided in inquiring about the child. I knew only that Eddie was a brother that did not live with us. And as time moved on, even this certainty became enmeshed in a fog.

Around the age of eleven, I bragged about Eddie's existence to a neighborhood boy. I still remember the idea of my confession being exotic and sure to shock the boy. He immediately questioned the voracity of my story, "You do not have a brother named Edward." I had not planned on this challenge or the unnerving use of the formal version of Eddie's name. I called to my mother in an adjoining room:

"Mom, isn't it true that I have a brother named Eddie?" The depth of her silence swallowed me whole. The boy glared at me with the certain glee of catching me in a lie.

In my early teenage years, I asked my mother about Eddie. We sat at the kitchen table. She confessed she had been to see him and what had happened was horrible. While holding him, he had spit on her repeatedly. She added in a voice deeply marked with grief that Eddie could not talk and he was severely retarded. Her pain was deep. This was the first time I had some hint of what she had endured. From this conversation I developed the idea of Eddie bound in some form of restraining garment partitioned in a white walled institutional room. I did not ask my mother about Eddie for another thirty years. I did not want to cause her any pain.

As the years passed there were more arguments and hostility between my parents. At times the arguments spilled out of the closed bedroom door. By the time I left home at eighteen, the house had become an emotionally cold place. I avoided being there as much as possible. Their inevitable divorce came eight years later.

***

As the State of Florida was expanding facilities for its handicapped residents, significant changes in public attitudes toward the mentally retarded came in the 1960s. With the election of a popular young president, John F. Kennedy, the public soon became aware of his sister confined to a mental institution in Wisconsin. Rosemary's condition cast light on a topic mostly left unspoken. Here was open acknowledgement and expressed love for a mentally retarded sister by the nation's president and his family. In 1961 Eunice Kennedy Shriver wrote an article in the Saturday Evening Post about Rosemary. These revelations by America's first family forced the country to rethink long held views regarding the mentally retarded and their treatment. During Kennedy's short term as president, he appointed several commissions and committees to investigate the status of the mentally retarded. In a 1963 address to congress he encouraged a goal "to retain in and return to the community the mentally ill and mentally retarded, and there to restore and revitalize their lives through better health programs and strengthened educational and rehabilitation services." Five years after the president's assassination, Mrs. Shriver created in 1968 The Special Olympics, bringing the mentally and physically handicapped onto neighborhood playing fields and into the hearts of many Americans. The smiling face of a Down syndrome child racing down a high school track became an iconic image of the Special Olympics in newspapers across the country.

This dialogue about mental retardation initiated and pushed many in the country to look a little differently at those with mental problems. Perhaps shutting people off in institutions was not the best way to go. Perhaps there were different ways to treat these people and bring them back on some level into society.

On 14 December 1965, six - year - old Eddie was transferred from Sunland Training Center in Gainesville to Marianna.

Eddie was fortunate to have landed at Marianna. Although the reform movement of State institutions had not taken hold of every facility in the country, Eddie was in a safe community of involved and motivated caretakers.

Years after Eddie's transfer to Sunland Marianna, I had a chance to tour the facility and meet with caregivers who had worked with my brother.

Carolyn Mayo a second - generation staff member at Sunland Marianna is rail thin with a head of stand up straight hair and a quick, beautiful smile. Her deeply lined face tells of a life of hard work. She is fiercely dedicated to the residents in her care and takes great pride in her contributions to Eddie's growth. Considering the hundreds of children she has cared for, her contribution to our society is immeasurable. The deep emotion in her voice, plaintive and at times cracking makes it obvious why residents call her and other caregivers, "Mama."

"At the time Eddie came here," Carolyn said, "they had institutional style furniture - state issue and I set out to get each of the twenty - three people in Harrison House their own beds, their own chest of drawers. Harrison House was the first house that got that accomplished. I used my Daddy's pickup truck to go and buy twin beds. I wanted the house to be homey.

"We had the learning center. Eddie would go there at nine in the morning and stay until eleven. The children were taught different skills, such as how to stuff silverware in a tray, and for those that did not comprehend very much they would stack rings on the cones. They would do whatever they could do for their abilities. They were learning skills...How to do something. Eddie learned to wad up the newspapers. We also continued the training that my Mother started, the activities of daily living: How to brush their teeth, how to comb their hair. Some of them might play basketball, might go outside and bounce a ball. Eddie loved to bounce a basketball."

Carolyn remembered Eddie as inquisitive and one who would participate fully in the events and activities. He would lie on his bed and sort through his belongings or straighten the clothes in his chest of drawers several times a day

"He loved to decorate the House on any holiday," Carolyn remembers. "Christmas. They all looked forward to everything decorated at Christmas. Eddie got right in and helped decorate. Halloween, it did not matter the holiday. Halloween carnivals were his favorite. He liked the masks. Big old rubber Frankenstein mask. He loved it. Eddie would come up and try to say, "boo!" One Halloween I put some soccer balls in a sheet and put them around the house and in the yard to make ghosts. Eddie got me by the hand. He had a sheet and he had a ball, and he had a shoelace, and I thought 'ok, what do you want?' He took me to his room…he wanted me to fix a ghost that was *his* ghost. Hang it over *his* bed. Eddie lacks the ability to talk but I knew by his gestures what he wanted. The shoelace was to wrap it around the sheet and make the head of the ghost. And I had to thumbtack it up like the ghost was flying right over his bed. Now that is how Eddie was. He was very smart. He could understand everything you said to him. He could dress himself. Feed himself. He liked music. Eddie could thread a belt where most of the residents could not. He could wear a suit and a tie. He liked to dress up. He liked to look nice. He knew he looked nice. Every Easter Eddie looked forward to church down at the park in the afternoon with the relatives that would come."

The staff and caregivers at Sunland Marianna in the late 1970s and 1980s were given options to introduce their charges to the world outside the spacious and beautiful grounds of Sunland. Trips to the beach to collect shells were a favorite activity. The Special Olympics offered the general public a chance to observe the potential of the mentally retarded. With buses loaded, staff and patients visited local zoos, shopping malls and the greatest adventure of all, trips to Disney World, five hours away.

Carolyn, her memory rekindled, adds, "Eddie loved the animals at the zoo. He loved the wild dog and cats around Sunland. He liked to see a small child; he just liked to tickle them. He had a thing about cars and vans; he liked to slam the doors.

"Back in the late 80s and 90s we had a little reward for citizen of the month. Eddie won. The award was put in a frame above his bed. The reward was based on how the individual might have done any number of things he or she was doing. Dressing, whatever. Any area where they made progress. Eddie's award was based on holding the door for a lady. He was very proud of that award."

In just a few minutes, Carolyn had described the significant changes Eddie and his fellow residents had experienced in a two - decade span. I asked Sunland Administrator Lucious Williams who had joined our discussion what else might have contributed to the betterment of the mentally handicapped.

"Let me give you one example," he said. "1975 that was the year the Bill of Rights was passed and that was significant. Before, there were corporeal punishments, spankings..."

"Tying them down when their behavior got bad," Carolyn adds.

The Developmentally Disabled Assistance and Bill of Rights Act of 1975 was an extraordinary piece of legislation. In addition to prohibiting corporeal punishment, the bill included rights to appropriate treatment in a setting least restrictive of the patient's liberty, to a well - balanced diet, to needed medical and dental services, to be free of excessive use of restraints, to be visited by relatives and to a safe environment. The Bill also required a return to normal community living whenever possible and education in public schools.

The Bill of Rights Act, (PL 94 - 103), went into effect in October of 1977. Eddie Burke was eighteen - years - old. The Bill's passage set into motion a sea change in treatment of the mentally handicapped.

Although few could understand the sweep of the Bill at the time, the possibilities opened to Eddie and others were astounding. In 1992, after spending almost thirty - three years in an evolving system of institutions he was given the opportunity to move out.

Lucious Williams is a handsome, deliberate man in his late fifties. When asked questions, he thinks carefully before answering. He has dedicated his life's work to the mentally handicapped. I was sitting in Lucious's office at a conference table. Joining us were Carolyn Mayo and Mary Huckaby, another of Sunland's caregivers who knew Eddie. I was curious how Eddie was able to leave Sunland Marianna.

"Social workers come and have a dialogue with our staff about skills," Lucious said. "What this person can do, what does each person need, and so forth. They then match up the resident's family's location and services offered. One of the goals is to get the residents physically close to their families. In Eddie's case, your family lived near St. Augustine. It was a process also of matching up skills. Our staff, after discussions with the social workers would say, 'this is a person who meets your requirements.' This process could be done in a matter of weeks, or at the most, a month."

"We did not make the decision which of the residents would be chosen," Carolyn adds. "The social worker might ask the staff what a resident could do, and then ask how that person could fit into the community. What could Eddie do in the community?"

"That dialogue is so important." Lucious said. "What kind of food does she like? Does he get upset easily? If so, what do you do?"

"We know how residents like Eddie are going to behave," Carolyn says. "There are residents here I can tell when they are going to have a seizure. We know by observing over the years. One of the questions asked would be, 'would he leave the area?' This was important information to pass along. We all want to make sure he or she fits in at the new home."

I asked Carolyn how difficult is it to say goodbye to someone like Eddie after so many years.

"It hurts. The ones we have seen leave, the ones that have passed away… It just blows me away. Because I get attached to them. I am attached to all of them." She hesitates a moment. "I've shed a lot of tears."

"Eddie Burke," Mary says, "understood he was leaving. He packed his clothes and was not upset at all. It was a status to get out...One thing you need to know. Eddie Burke was loved here."

On 18 May 1992, Eddie Burke climbed into the back of a car and was driven to the Williams - Young House in St. Augustine, Florida. Making this transition with Eddie was another Sunland Marianna resident, George. George also had family near St. Augustine. Eddie was a thirty - two years old severely impaired Down syndrome man. He had lived much of his life in State institutions.

***

In the years since Eddie was removed from our home, I had never had one conversation with my father about him and if my middle brother and I ever discussed Eddie, I do not remember it.

My mother, however, unknown to any of us, had been in constant contact with the care - givers at both Sunland Gainesville and Sunland Marianna as Eddie's legal guardian. She sent Eddie money, clothes, gifts and photographs of his brothers and parents.

The one thing she did not do, though, after the spitting incident was to visit Eddie. On some level she must have known Eddie was a far different person than the six - year - old who repeatedly spat upon her. In reading the yearly and medical reports she would have understood, as I later did reading the same papers, that Eddie was capable of far greater and positive interaction with others.

As legal guardian, Betty would have been aware of Eddie's transfer. After her divorce from my father, she lived alone in a small home she had designed and built just north of St. Augustine, living on a meager income provided by accounting and personal administrative work for several wealthy individuals in the nearby golfing community of Ponte Vedra Beach. She was outgoing, funny and vivacious when around people but due to circumstances of her own design, spent long hours and days even, without seeing another person. Eddie's transfer to St. Augustine was no random decision. One of the goals of the social workers and the staff at

Sunland Marianna was to send residents to a facility near family.

Whether she was anxious or excited about Eddie's move I do not know. I am willing to bet, however, that she drove to the Williams - Young House on 18 May 1992 and parked her car within sight of the front door, eyes scanning the half - circle parking lot for the vehicle delivering her third son to his new home.

***

In the late 1990s, my mother asked me to purchase several Celine Dion cassette tapes. I did not expect my mother to be a fan of the Canadian singer. Her musical tastes ran more to Ray Charles, Lyle Lovett, Linda Ronstadt and the rhythmic swing music of her youth. When I expressed surprise at her musical choice, she told me the tapes were not for her but for Eddie. Someone had indicated on a report mailed to her of Eddie's love of Dion's music.

I went to the local Target and purchased four Celine Dion cassettes. I gave these to my mother without asking the obvious questions. I remember thinking it strange that someone who was so profoundly mentally impaired would express an interest in music. But like all things "Eddie" I chose to not ask any questions. I was wrong not to have done so. How clear it is now that my mother could have easily stopped by the store and purchased the music herself. Yet she asked me to do it. I completely missed her message.

Betty's terminal cancer diagnosis came in June of 2004. Months later while driving her to a radiation treatment, she casually mentioned that we should go see Eddie sometime. She said he lived not too far away. Perhaps the reality of her condition had prompted this idea. The cancer had moved with frightening speed from the chest wall and lung into several of her ribs, breaking each as the tumors progressed. She was in constant pain and losing weight. I mumbled agreement that we should go see him. But I never pursued it. At that stage of her disease I did not want anything to upset her. We never traveled the few miles south together to see her third child.

***

One year after receiving a diagnosis of lung cancer, Betty Whitlow Burke died on July 19, 2005. She was seventy - seven years old.

Several days later, I began the process of cleaning her home. I started in her bathroom tossing decades of accumulated shampoos and cleaners into the trash before scrubbing the sink and tub. Bathroom completed, I moved into the closet of her bedroom. Her clothes hung neatly from thick plastic hangers. Pushing aside hanging coats and blouses, I found deep in the corner of the closet the small floor safe with a heavy, unlocked lid. I rummaged through the safe's contents. At the very bottom was an old, green hanging folder. Inside the folder were two manila folders. Each was thick and had the identical words written in ballpoint pen ink on the worn tabs: "Eddie Burke." I tossed the files onto her bed and retrieved a Coke from the kitchen. My plan was to take a quick break from cleaning and thumb through the documents. I spread the contents on the bed and began to read.

Two hours later I stood, slightly dizzy and overwhelmed. The contents of the two folders covered the entire bed. I was done for the day. In fact, it was early in the afternoon with plenty of time and light to work but I was stunned by what I had read. I was unable to do anymore. The bottle of Coke was warm and untouched.

With the two folders secure under my arm, I locked up her house and headed home.

That night, I rearranged her papers in chronological order to help make sense of Eddie's life. Items pertaining to Eddie's birth and earlier years included thin, translucent carbon copies of letters written by his pediatrician ("I am writing to you in regards to Edward M. Burke, one month old mongoloid son of…"), the February 25th 1960 Presbyterian Tidings newsletter announcing

Eddie's birth, copies of his birth certificate, yellow faded newspaper clipping listing "new Births at Baptist Hospital," a "There Can Be Strength in Tragedy" article carefully torn from a 1960 magazine called Home, the letter from Sunland Training Center at Gainesville accepting Eddie as a patient. There was a long, nearly illegible handwritten letter from a Miss Gault, a nurse and later Dean of the Nursing School of Vanderbilt responding to the news that Eddie was to be placed outside the home.

"My dear..." the letter begins. "...You and Herb have made your decision in the light of many complexities and you have done what seemed best for all concerned and from this distance it seems sound. Your two little boys need you very much, my dear, and Herb needs your support and all that you can do for him in these months that are undoubtedly the most difficult in his professional career as he builds his practice in a new community."

While Eddie was at Sunland Training Centers in Gainesville and Marianna there is very little State of Florida provided documentation, mainly Betty's extensive writings describing her pain, torment, anger and guilt. Once Eddie moved out of State run institutions to the Williams - Young House operated by The Arc of the St. Johns in St. Augustine, the amount of information on his well being increased dramatically. It was among these papers describing his day - to - day life and ability to function well with others that I found reason to find my brother. I was puzzled why my mother did not go to Eddie after reading comments such as, "Eddie is a friendly outgoing young man who...Is gifted with a positive attitude...And who likes to be helpful and always jumps right in to lend a hand...He likes to keep things neat..." from The Arc's August 2003 Annual Support Plan Update. Was the pain too deep for her to establish a relationship with her third son? It is clear from the reports, Eddie was functioning at a level much higher than I had imagined.

Made clear in the files was my mother's unresolved anger at my father from the time of Eddie's birth through the remaining years of the marriage, contributing to its demise. In one of her journal entries, she documents secrets Herb had kept from her. Number one on the two - page, single spaced document was *he was in the delivery room with me...but did not tell me (about Eddie's condition). I discovered that myself when I first looked at Eddie the morning after he was born.*

The files containing my mother's journals and letters are the best indication of her suffering. My guilt is equal or even greater to the guilt of my family members. There were those few, rare and unguarded times when my mother told me Eddie was living in Gainesville, then Marianna and finally St. Augustine. I remember thinking I should go see him on my own but soon forgot the idea. Perhaps I did not want the burden of opening up a relationship with someone mentally disabled, someone who could only spit. My last opportunity, in 2004, to visit Eddie at my mother's request came as she was dying. I failed again at doing what would have been the right thing.

***

It was time to correct my own failings. I looked up The Arc (Association of Retarded Citizens) of the St. Johns online and fired off an email to the Executive Director, Kathy Jackson.

"Dear Kathy,

5 August 2005

My name is Andy Burke. I am the eldest son of Betty Burke and the oldest brother of Eddie Burke. My Mother passed away several weeks ago on 19 July. I spent the afternoon reading through her files on Eddie and would appreciate some guidance from you or someone on you staff as to what steps I should be taking regarding Eddie. I live in Jacksonville Beach and would welcome an appointment with whomever you suggest.

Thank you in advance,

Andy Burke"

Less than an hour later, I received a response:

"Dear Andy,

I'm sorry to hear that your Mom passed away. I don't know if any of our folks knew. I would be more than happy to meet with you to discuss Eddie. He has been with us for many years and has been a delight. He's well liked by our staff and he's so full of life. Please let me know when you would like to come down...I look forward to meeting you and hope that I can help with any questions you might have.

Kathy Jackson"

The Arc of the St. Johns is located off Interstate I - 95 near the nation's oldest city of St. Augustine, Florida. Situated less than ten miles from its namesake river, The Arc of the St. Johns is one of more than eight hundred and fifty such organizations scattered throughout the U.S. Founded in 1950 by a group of concerned parents, The Arc is dedicated to providing a safe and healthy living and working environment to children and adults with intellectual and developmental disabilities. With a guiding philosophy of looking at the person first as "individuals we serve," The Arc is active politically in assuring that those people with mental disabilities are represented and protected at the local, State and National levels. There are approximately 100 people working as staff at The Arc of the St. Johns serving 120 individuals with disabilities. Led by Kathy and her predecessors, The Arc of the St. Johns has won awards for the varied amount of services offered to the community. As a State funded entity, The Arc must abide by HUD's guidelines on residents and community clients served.

In addition to offering its individuals a place to work and learn through its Industrial Training Center with educational and art classes, The Arc owns and operates eight residential houses throughout St. Johns County.

The receptionist led me to Kathy's office. Kathy stood to greet me. She smiled warmly and with a sweep of her arm indicated a chair for me. Her desk was the desk of a busy person. Organized, yet supporting islands of projects.

"It is a real pleasure to meet you at last," she said, eyes alive and bright. "We do not have this happen often. At least not often enough."

Kathy's exuberance and excitement about my visit alleviated any slight concerns or misgivings I had preceding my visit. Here was an energetic, determined woman engaged in doing something she felt was important.

Kathy took time asking me questions about my family and my background. She mentioned that we lived in the same Jacksonville Beach neighborhood. Her warmth made me comfortable. At some point, I turned the conversation to the reasons I was there.

"Yes, I am curious about that myself," she said. "We have not had too many cases like this. It is very exciting for all of us that you are here."

I recounted my only memory of Eddie in the crib and living a life shadowed by an awareness and guilt knowing I had a young brother ensconced in institutions in Gainesville and later Marianna. He could only spit and I should never bring up Eddie's name in front of my father and if I did so with my mother, it would cause her pain. And like a confession and an apology rolled into one long narrative, I related finding the journals and contacting my middle brother and questioning my own motives for wanting to meet Eddie.

As I related my story, Kathy leaned forward, listening carefully. Her attention assisted me in getting it all out. She was interested in Eddie and his life story. I was filling in some of the blanks. I spoke of everything I could that would aid us both in providing a platform for a successful relationship with Eddie.

"There is a case very similar to your family's. They live nearby as well. And like Eddie, their child, a boy, was taken away about the same time and age as Eddie was. He was placed in Sunland at the insistence of the father. And like your story, the family was dissuaded from discussing or visiting the child. This attitude was very common in the fifties and sixties. So when the father passed away not too long ago, the mother and her family took the now grown man home to live with them. It was the way things were done back then. The way many fathers thought about the families as a whole. It was considered better to place the special child in an institution or facility."

I told Kathy the three fields analogy given to my mother by Dr. Lanier.

"That is the way it was viewed. The medical profession believed they were doing what was best for everybody. Now we have a far different approach. These days, children under 18 cannot be legally placed away from the home. Eddie spends his time here at The Arc working until three o'clock then he, along with about one hundred and twenty individuals we serve, board buses to take them to their respective homes or as we call them, Houses. Eddie lives at the Williams - Young House not too far from here. It is the largest of our houses, with twelve individuals living there.

"Are you ready to meet your brother?" Kathy asked. I was ready and appreciative to Kathy for the way she handled our discussion. "Just remember Eddie cannot communicate as we do but he is a smart man and understands how to let us know what he wants."

Kathy led me down a long hallway. Off each side of the hallway were spacious rooms full of clients taking classes, doing art or working. She greeted co - workers and clients in the same friendly, open manner. Frankly at times, it was difficult for me to tell who was who so I greeted all in the same manner: "Hey, how's it is going?" Some would respond; others simply stared. A few of the people I encountered had obvious physical characteristics of the severely impaired. All people I passed looked at me with great curiosity. Here was a new face. The staff had heard about the family member visiting his brother for the first time. Perhaps they also knew the history of our family's inattention to Eddie as he lived his life. If the staff knew this history, they held no outward grudge toward me. I was welcomed as family. Some of the staff stopped me.

"Oh, you are Eddie's brother," a typical comment would go. "He is such a wonderful guy. You will love him."

One of the clients approached. He was short and compact with quick, rapid movements. He reached out to shake hands and in doing so pulled me toward him. His eyes jumped wildly, sometimes resting on my own. "How are YOOOOOOO?" he asked. "Good! Good! Good!" he replied before I could answer. Then he was off on another adventure.

It was an interesting, sometimes raucous three - minute walk.

By the time Kathy and I exited the main building into the hot August day and back into the air conditioning of an annex building, a group of staff and clients were trailing behind us. As we entered the building, another staff member greeted me. Kathy introduced Janet Pratt. I looked around the room. There were perhaps thirty people milling about, some watching a wall - mounted TV, others in chairs or at tables, some standing, staring out blankly. The room was clean. Sunlight poured through large windows. A beautiful young woman illuminated by a bright wedge of light squatted against a far wall. She rocked herself, eyes fixed downward and arms clasped tightly around bended knees. She should be at the beach with friends or on her way to check out her college dorm room with her parents. She was fascinating to watch and it was an effort to pull my eyes away. What had she endured?

"Would you like to meet your brother?" Janet asked. With a nod of her head, she motioned to a man sitting at a desk. The desk was against a wall next to a window. "That is Eddie's place. His desk. Where he does his work." My brother's back was to us. His hair was close cropped, a mixture of grey and brown. Without trepidation, I approached him.

"Eddie," Janet said. He turned from his task of assembling plastic parts. "This is your brother Andy." Edward Morgan Burke looked at me. His eyes were slightly crossed and greenish brown, the color of my father's eyes. His face was thick skinned and consistent in appearance with physical characteristics of a Down syndrome individual. His ears were rounded and low on his head. He rose from his seat and stepped very close to me, looking up into my face, his head shifting from side to side as if to get proper bearing on the new person in front of him. He grabbed my hand and held it. His large tongue lolled out and he emitted a loud, extended grunt that ended with a hiccup - like vocalization.

"That means he is excited," Janet quickly explained. "Happy."

"Hello Eddie," I said. "How are you?"

He responded with a series of staccato hoots, concluding with an intake of air and another hoot.

"I think he recognizes you as his brother," a staff person said. I did not believe this but appreciated the excitement in her statement. Most in the room now were watching Eddie and me.

Here in front of me was a brother I did not know. I looked into his face trying to see some family resemblance, but beyond his eyes, there was none. We continued to hold hands. I did not know what the staff expected. I did not know what I expected from my first moments with Eddie. I felt responsibility for him but no real emotional connection. I knew on some level I would be a part of his life but did not know how much of my own life I could give him. I smiled and talked to him, asking the same question in different ways: "How are you? What are you doing? How have you been?" We stood holding hands for many minutes. Someone brought out a camera. He hooted when the flash went off. Then as quickly as he had risen to greet us, Eddie released my hand, turned and sat at his desk. He was ready to return to his work. I stood behind him watching his movements, looking at his hands, smallish and wrinkled, as he assembled the pieces of colorful plastic. I looked at the back of his head and his shoulders. His shoulders were rounded, his neck strong. These were perhaps the best moments of my visit. Eddie accepted my presence as he worked. I watched my brother. Then, it seemed, I heard for the first time the blaring of the TV. Had someone turned the volume up?

"OK," I said.

"Eddie, say goodbye to your brother," Janet said.

He turned and in the only vocalization I understood said, "bu, bu, bu, bu, bu…" He fanned the fingers of his right hand against his palm.

"Bye - bye Eddie, I'll see you soon," I said, patting him on the back.

I stopped in Kathy's office before leaving.

I asked about Eddie's eyesight. It seemed he could not see very well. His eyes were crossed and he squinted frequently. He would also hold up his right hand inches from his eyes and turn it over as if examining each pore and hair.

"He does need glasses," she responded, "but he will not wear them. We have taken him to an ophthalmologist for an examination and prescription. When fitted with glasses, he removes them and refuses to wear them at all. It is frustrating."

"One of the staff indicated Eddie recognized me as his brother. Is it possible?"

"Well, blood is thicker than water. This is where the teacher comes out in them. There is a connection…Not something you can see but I think he may have recognized you as his brother. I really do."

I realized I had taken too much of this busy person's time and thanked her for the kind reception she and her staff had provided. She walked me to the front door.

"We hope to see more of you. It means so much to Eddie and to all of us. This has been a very special day."

What had I expected of the visit? After reading the files I knew Eddie would not be sitting in the far corner of a padded room. He was cared for and doing jobs that gave him some sense of accomplishment. He was loved, fed, given shelter, clothed and safe.

The third farmer's field, a field that loomed so large in my parent's decision and in the medical culture of the 1950s and 60s, had been well tended by others. Crops had been sown and reaped year after year until forty - six years after being yanked dying from a crib, resuscitated then sent away to a series of homes and institutions, Edward Morgan Burke had come face to face with his oldest brother. He held my hand and looked into my eyes and expressed wonderment. After some minutes, he sat down at his desk. He had work that needed to be completed. A sense of wonder of my own crept over me as I drove home. There would be quite a story to tell my wife. I had done the right thing. A little late but it was there, this thing I had done.

* * *

One day Kathy Jackson called me. Her typical enthusiastic voice was pumped even higher.

"I just spoke with a colleague of mine and you have to meet with him. The similarities in your lives are striking. He is my counterpart of The Arc in Gainesville. His name is Dick Bradley."

Several weeks later I met with Dick in his office. He is the Executive Director and CEO of an agency serving four hundred developmentally disabled individuals in twenty - five Houses across Alachua County. A tall, serious man with a mass of graying hair, Dick listened as I explained my family's history. He had heard mine and similar stories before. In fact, he had lived the story although in his case, his narrative and a follow up correspondence related an unexpected and fortunate turn.

PART TWO

Richard (Dick) Bradley

Kathy Bradley

On July 21, 1955 in Ft. Myers, Florida the fourth child, of what ultimately would be seven, Kathleen Ann (Kathy) was born to Dr. James L. and Ann P. Bradley. It was immediately apparent because of her physical characteristics she had Down Syndrome.

Her older brother Jim Jr. was almost ten years old; I was three months shy of eight; and Roger was three and a half. Subsequently, brothers Christopher arrived in 1958, Brian in 1959, and a sister Carolyn in 1962. This large, Irish Catholic family would have important implications in Kathy's life for the next 60 years - as she would in theirs.

To understand the context of Kathy's birth it is helpful to consider various aspects of our culture, the State of Florida, the state of medical knowledge and practice, contemporary services and support for people with Intellectual and Developmental Disabilities (I/DD) in 1955 - as well as our parents' disposition toward their first daughter.

With regard to the culture in 1955, people with I/DD were, for the most part, invisible. They were not in the schools, on our playgrounds, in the workplace, and generally in any public venue. Many were institutionalized at a very early age. In fact, the prevailing belief among "professionals" was to put a child with I/DD in an institution as early as possible as he/she would be a disruptive influence on the family if remaining at home. If allowed to stay home, even for a short period, families would begin to "bond" with the child which would serve only to make the inevitable placement that much more difficult. In the "beat the Russians" 1950's very high value was placed on math, science, and achievement in general and little to none on "deficient" babies.

At that time the State of Florida was very much part of the Old South. The population of the old Confederacy was generally poorer, less well educated, more rural, and because of a variety of factors (including a less than robust tax base) provided less than adequate social services and support. This was especially true of services and supports for people with Intellectual and Developmental Disabilities and their families. To some extent that remains the case today since until recently Florida has ranked 49th among the 50 states in "fiscal effort" according to the Coleman Institute at the University of Colorado – the gold standard for these statistics for more than forty years.

The only state funded services for individuals with I/DD in Florida in 1955 was in Gainesville and then known as Sunland Center. Originally opened in 1921 as The Florida Farm Colony for the Epileptic and Feeble Minded, it now carries the name Tacachale (from pre - Columbian Timucua local Native American tribe meaning "lighting new fire.") The options available then for a family surprised by the birth of an intellectually disabled child were placement in this state institution, placement in a private home of some sort paid for by the family or have the child stay home with the family. The typical advice of the medical community at that time was to place the child as soon as possible (The Burkes). Having the child stay at home (The Bradleys) was rare.

A decision concerning these limited living options was exacerbated by the fact that the State was not required and did not provide educational services to severally disabled children. In the U.S.A. this began to change in the 1970's. In the 1972 case

Pennsylvania Association for Retarded Children (PARC) v. Commonwealth of Pennsylvania, the U.S. District court decided that a state could not deny, delay, or end any intellectually disabled student's access to a public education. The decision was reached after the Pennsylvania Board of Education, thirteen school districts, and the state's secretaries of education and public welfare sued the Commonwealth of Pennsylvania. The opinion asserted that education should be viewed as a continuous process focused not only on academics but also on teaching students how to manage their surroundings. Similarly, in Mills v. Board of Education of District of Columbia, a case decided the same year, a group of students labeled "mentally retarded, emotionally disturbed or hyperactive" by D.C. public schools filed a civil action suit against the school system after being denied admission without due process under the Equal Protection Clause of the Fourteenth Amendment. The court condemned the school's decision and declared that all children in D.C., regardless of any physical, mental, or emotional disabilities, are entitled to a free and appropriate public education. In 1975 Congress passed Public Law 94 - 142, also known as the Education for All Handicapped Children Act, which outlined that public schools should provide all students with an education appropriate for their unique needs at public expense.

With regard to our parents' temperament at the time, some of this is speculation based upon history, background, religion and subsequent events. I remember our parents telling Jim, Roger, and me that God had given us Kathy because he was confident we would take good care of her and "do the right thing". Being devout Irish Catholic our parents did consider this a pre - ordained birth.

Our father, Dr. James (Jim) Bradley, was the only child of a housewife and a mail clerk on the New York Central Railroad from the Village of Lyons, New York. His parents were one generation removed from Ireland and their parents had brought the strong attachments to Catholicism and family that were typical of the 19th century immigrants from that island. Additionally, Lyons was a very small, working class village with the work ethic and family values one would expect in such a setting in the early 20th Century. These characteristics were inculcated in him as a child and probably influenced the family's decision following Kathy's birth.

Jim would be the first in his family to go to college. His math wizardry would get him a scholarship to Cornell University and his success there landed him admission to Yale Medical School from which he graduated in 1944 and began a specialty in surgery. He, as was his entire fifty member Yale class, immediately inducted into the U.S. Army Medical Corps since World War II was still raging. Shortly before reporting for duty, he married Ann Perkins.

Ann (Perkins) Bradley was the only child of a senior executive of a large chemical company. After graduating from Syracuse University with a degree in Sociology she enrolled in Yale School of Nursing and earned a Master's degree. Given her father's position with an international company she had traveled the world extensively. As was Jim's, this was a very loving, close knit family of only three.

Ann's parents, being quite well to do, would play an important role following the birth of Kathy. Ann's father, Richard H. Perkins, would assume an important role in The Arc of Lee County (then called LARC) and would establish a trust fund for Kathy. His and his wife's donations, supplemented over time by our parents, would ultimately result in quite a large fund. This ultimately allowed a maximum amount of freedom and choice throughout Kathy's life.

Following the death of Ann's parents, their Caloosahatchee River front home in North Ft. Myers would be donated by Ann to The Arc of Lee County for use as a group home in 1991. It is situated directly across from downtown Ft. Myers where the river is about a mile wide. It is still in use as such today.

(Subsequent note: The Home was flooded with more than five - feet of water inside during Category 4 Hurricane Ian in September, 2022. Since repairs would cost more than 50% of the value of the home, current building codes require it be raised a considerable height. Doing so is just not economically feasible. The LARC Board of Directors has therefore decided to take the insurance payout, sell the property and use the proceeds to build a new home on land it owns in Cape Coral.)

Interestingly, Jim and Ann Bradley, both having been only children, would ultimately have seven of their own. These children were born beginning in 1945 and the last arrived in January of 1962. Kathy was right in the middle having been born in 1955. Both had wanted siblings and the number of children produced by this union was probably a result of the strong Catholic faith, lack of meaningful birth control at the time and their experience of being only children themselves. In any event, Ann was known to have opined on occasion that, "If anyone ever tells you the "rhythm method" works they don't know what they are talking about and I have several examples to prove it." All of their children will tell you they absolutely loved being in a large family. It is quite telling that Jim and Ann had three more children following the birth of Kathy.

These background descriptions are provided to show these parents of a child with a severe intellectual disability were very well educated people with a somewhat extensive knowledge of the world. Despite this they knew very little indeed about Kathy's condition, its implications, and what resources might be available for her and for them.

Given their extensive connections in the medical world, including mentors and others at Yale and other notable teaching hospitals, our parents began an extensive inquiry into Down Syndrome - its implications, treatments if any, and services and supports for the child and the family. What they found was not encouraging. Since Kathy was clearly a "classic case of severe Down Syndrome" they were told she would probably never progress past the mental age of two or three, never be able to perform very basic self - care skills, go to school or be unsupervised. Almost universally they were told to institutionalize her as soon as possible because she would most certainly be a "disruptive influence on the family". In the end, none of these predictions would come to define the life of Kathy Bradley.

As a result of these investigations and consultations, they researched and visited a number of private homes for children such as Kathy as well as the only state institution for them existing at the time in Gainesville.

Our parents, and particularly Mom, were not excited by what they found in Gainesville. With no Interstate Highway in Florida at that time it also would have been about a five hour drive from Ft. Myers. Nonetheless, the insistent and ubiquitous advice they were given continued to be to place Kathy as soon as possible for her benefit as well as for the family's. In any event, at that time there were no vacancies for infants and very young children in Gainesville. The institution placed Kathy on a waiting list. As it turned out this was truly a blessing in disguise.

***

As an aside, I think it is important for the reader to know what state institutions were like years ago. You will find later in this book I began a professional career in service to people with intellectual disabilities in 1974 at the Sunland Center in Ft. Myers as a direct care worker - a "Resident Training Instructor". (Note that this was about 18 years after my sister Kathy would have been admitted to the Gainesville Sunland.) Since my only real experience with people with these disabilities prior to this was with my sister the contrast was surreal. I believe it was at this time that I truly understood how profoundly important my family's decision to keep Kathy at home rather than place her in the institution really was.

Because the facility needed someone 'big and strong" I was assigned to a cottage of 40 profoundly mentally handicapped young women who exhibited some very aggressive and destructive behaviors. The dayroom where they spent most of their day was a rectangular room about 40 feet by 25 feet. Furniture consisted of one wooden picnic table bolted to the floor. The 40 women all dressed in state issue white tee shirts and green shorts milled aimlessly about in various stages of undress. Very few had much in the way of self - care and toileting skills creating a strong odor of urine and feces. There was a discernible pecking order among them and avoidance of the more aggressive was clearly important. I vividly remember one woman who was a severe biter who staked out a corner of the room wherein none of the others would approach her. She would stand, snatch flies out of the air, and pop them in her mouth and eat them. To say I was shocked by this scene would be the epitome of understatement. It was in the dictionary sense incredible...Impossible to believe.

I do not want the reader left with the impression this was the case in all parts of the institution nor that it was the result of a completely indifferent staff. First, consider that these 40 women typically had a staff on duty of 3, 4 at best. At least one had to be in the bathroom at all times and another doing administrative chores in the office area or kitchen /dinning - setting up medications, making appointments, preparing /cleaning the dining area, doing laundry, etc. This left two people to watch 40 completely dependent women and try to intervene in the mayhem that frequently broke out. Again, just an incredible and difficult situation. I know many of the staff cared about these individuals but the task was really just impossible. Certainly, no opportunity to teach these individuals any self - care, daily living, or social skills existed. There were certainly many wonderful people functioning as caregivers – they were simply overwhelmed. Secondly, as one moved through the cottages to more and more capable individuals, conditions improved as the residents were able to do more and more for themselves.

These horrendous conditions were primarily the direct result of the absolutely minimal State of Florida funding for these services and facilities. It was not until the Federal government began assisting the states (through the Medicaid ICF/DD program which began in Florida in a limited way at Ft. Myers Sunland in 1975) these conditions began to dramatically improve as a result of additional staff, Federal requirements for "Active Treatment", and building construction/renovation standards which came attached to the extra dollars.

***

Our parents were determined to make the waiting period as positive as they could. Having been told in Gainesville that the more Kathy could do for herself by the time a vacancy became available the better her life there would be, they sought to have our family teach her as much as possible in the self - care realm. Wisely, they enlisted her three older brothers in this effort. We were told that Kathy could eventually learn everything that we had learned, albeit it would take her longer and everyone would have to help. For the next two years that is exactly what happened and she did begin to learn the fundamentals of feeding and dressing herself as well as rudimentary play with others.

In any event after about two years our parents were notified by the facility in Gainesville that Kathy had reached the top of the waiting list and that she could now be admitted. I am not sure exactly what our parents' thought process was at the time but I do know that they decided to present a question to me and my two brothers. The question, which had profound consequences for Kathy and for the family, was simply, "Should we place Kathy in the facility in Gainesville or should she stay home with us?" This question was posed, as most things were in our family, to the three older brothers seated around the small, intimate breakfast nook table in our kitchen. The question was posed in an entirely opened ended fashion - there were no value statements or leading phrases of any kind included. Just simply should she stay or should she go?

After two plus years of living, playing, and helping with Kathy it is both fair and accurate to say that we had clearly bonded with her. She was loving, happy and playful - and our only sister. I am pretty sure that it was Roger, then about six years old, who first spoke up and forcefully stated he wanted her to stay home with us. Oldest brother Jim and I quickly followed suit. The truth is it was a very short meeting. The only additional discussion was a reminder to us kids that this was going to require effort and participation from all of us. We all eagerly agreed and the die was cast. It was stressed again that she could learn but that it would simply take her longer to do so.

With the participation of all, Kathy stayed home with us and slowly but methodically learned various basic skills, rudimentary communication techniques and our rhythms of home and family life - not unlike any typical child just more slowly. Importantly, in addition to the efforts to teach her to do for herself at home, she was included in all family activities - Sunday Mass, trips to the store, going to restaurants, the swim club, trips to the beach, vacations to the mountains, the brothers ' sporting events like Little League and Pop Warner football. I do not think we knew it at the time but this is precisely how all kids learning is expanded through experiential participation. Had she been in the state institution in Gainesville she would have participated in none of these activities.

Having three very active brothers resulted in Kathy being a definite tomboy. Early on she became an outstanding swimmer (when at the beach she also excelled at body surfing and "boogie" boarding) and gleefully participated in our neighborhood games of tag, football, baseball, bike riding and exploring. As always, it was our parents' expectation that we participate with Kathy and that she participate with us which resulted in her never being left behind when we interacted with the neighborhood kids. Our bond with her continued to grow as we would not let her be excluded and woe unto any other kid who would dare to make fun of her. Her three brothers were there to make sure she was treated the same as we were. Unlike other people in the world in general at that time having similar conditions, there was absolutely no making fun of Kathy Bradley among the kids in our neighborhood! As the three older brothers left home for college, the next two brothers and eventually her sister continued to involve her in much of what they did and continued the tradition of not letting anyone disparage Kathy at any time for any reason.

Older brother Jim remembers an incident which highlights Kathy's athletic prowess. He recalls one afternoon Mom Bradley got a call from the principal of what would become The Arc of Lee County's school when Kathy was about 10 years old. She called to let mom know that Kathy was teaching the other kids at the school how to play basketball. The principal asked, "Where did she learn that?" Mom's matter - of - fact reply? "Kathy has three older brothers that play basketball with her all the time."

***

In 1950, five years before Kathy's birth, what is now The Arc of the United States was founded in New York by a small group of parents determined that their children should have the same opportunities in life that "typical" children have. In 1954 a similarly small group of parents in Ft. Myers founded a local chapter of The Arc (LARC - for Lee County Arc).

These local parents believed their children had an inherent right to an education through the public school system which was supported by their tax dollars just as any other child of parents in the community did. They began to fund raise for a school for their children and they negotiated with the School Board of Lee County to provide a teacher if the parents provided the classroom space. Riverside School, a small school (7 children), was started in1954 located at Riverside Baptist Church. The church graciously offered their classroom building during the week at no cost. The Lee County School Board, with Louise Farney as the Coordinator of Special Education, chose James Parrish to be the teacher for three hours per day. The School Board furnished Mr. Parrish's salary and the Shriner's Club of Fort Myers, of which Kathy's grandfather Richard Perkins was a member, furnished all the equipment and supplies for the school.

Riverside School quickly outgrew these facilities and the parent organization approached the Lee County Commission for help. The Commission offered a room and porch (one half of a porch) at the old caretakers building at Terry Park. Funds were needed to remodel the facilities into serviceable classrooms. The community responded with a total of $2,500 and the remodeling was carried out in September of 1956. Twenty intellectually disabled children were enrolled with one teacher, Ms. Annie Lee Johnson, paid by the School Board and one aide, Bertha Eady, paid by LARC. Through the influence of Kathy's grandfather Perkins the benevolence of the Fort Myers Shrine Club continued to furnish classroom equipment and supplies.

LARC is mentioned because as a family it was important to us but more importantly to show that our family situation was not unique in our community. There were several families looking to provide solutions for educating their children who did not meet the State's IQ standards - where a "sound mind" was required for public school attendance. A "sound mind" was defined by the State as an IQ of 50 points or above. These families did not do it alone. It also took the Ft. Myers community to support the needs of these families and Ft. Myers in the 1950's was small enough that people pretty much knew everyone else and knew who those families were. They were their friends and neighbors.

As Fort Myers' population ballooned in 1959 came also the need for more space and teachers for the school. To accomplish this the School Board would lease the land at Hanson and Evans Streets if LARC could raise $25,000 from the community for the construction of the school building. There was to be ample space for 30 children and a staff of three or four teachers.

Instruction would be offered in simple arts and crafts and everyday living skills. The community again responded to LARC by not only meeting the $25,000 goal to build the school, but by topping the goal by another $5,000 in donations plus labor and materials amounting to another $20,000 for a total of $50,000. The Riverside School became a reality and held Open House in the Fall of 1960 with Annie Lee Johnson & Barbara Vandercook as teachers in a two classroom building with a small kitchen and cafeteria. There were 21 children ages 6 to 17 enrolled in the school. Four more joined the group within a week.

***

Kathy began attending The Riverside School in 1960 when she was five years old. LARC grew over the years to provide a variety of life span services/supports and productive work programs. Kathy would continue to participate in its 'programs for fifty five years until her death in January, 2015 at the age of 60.

Just as our Mom told us many times over the years, Kathy was able to learn a variety of life skills even though her measured IQ was in the neighborhood of 25 - 30. It took her longer but she acquired many functional self - care, daily living, and social skills. I have encountered many, many individuals over my 40 - plus years of professional experience in services to people with I/DD who had a similar IQ level and who had been placed in an institution at a young age but in many respects required almost total care. This is the starkest and most poignant manner in which the difference between being institutionally placed and growing with a family can be demonstrated for me. To illustrate I can describe a typical day in her mid to late adult life at home, work, and play:

The night before a work day, Kathy would make and pack her lunch for the next day and set her own alarm clock. While I am not sure how she might have conceptualized time, I know she had an acute functional sense of when things were supposed to happen and what that looked like on a clock. When the alarm went off, she would get up, make her own breakfast, do her basic hygiene, pick out her clothes, and dress herself. As she ate breakfast she would 'read' the newspaper in a fashion which she apparently picked from our Dad. She always had it open to the stock market page – I suppose she was checking the performance and status of her Trust account! When I observed this I would question her as to how her portfolio was doing and she typically would simply respond, "Good."

She would catch the bus and go to LARC for her job in the wood shop where workers made survey stakes and shipping pallets. While her duties there changed over the years they included running an industrial saw, assembling pallets, and packing stakes in bundles. She absolutely loved her job and paycheck. She was always incredibly proud to show to her family that she was a productive and contributing member of society. As with most people with jobs in a team environment, her co - workers were some of her closest friends and she derived a great deal of social capital from her relationships with them. I could tell how close they were and how much she enjoyed them by observing their interactions at break times, lunch, and at quitting time.

She earned vacation time with the job and Mom Bradley would play hell trying to get her to take a vacation each summer to a camp in Orlando for two weeks. She was always very worried that if she was gone she would lose her job - despite the fact this was earned vacation time and her older brother Roger was the CEO of the organization!! Despite our constant reassurances, her job was so important to her that she was never comfortable with the idea of being gone. Fortunately, when she actually got to camp she enjoyed the activities and her friends from prior years and generally had a great time. Nonetheless, the next year was always characterized by the same job loss anxiety.

After work she caught the bus home and let herself in with her key. As Dad had passed away and Mom volunteered at a variety of places and was frequently not home at that time of the afternoon, having her own key provided Kathy more responsibility. Once home Kathy would always do her exercise program. She usually spent about an hour on her exercise bicycle and would swim a specified number of laps in the pool - kept track with pennies which would be transferred from one end to the other at the end of each lap. She would eat dinner with Mom, the only meal of the day she did not prepare for herself. Occasionally, when Mom was out for the evening, dinner would have been placed in the microwave oven with an appropriate amount of cooking time already entered and Kathy would push the start button to "zap 'it for herself.

Evenings were spent watching her favorite TV shows and knitting. Over the years these included Lawrence Welk (which she would help Mr. Welk conduct with her own conductor's baton), Lost in Space, Mork and Mindy, Star Trek, Andy Griffith, and Hawaii 5 - 0 among others. An exceptional favorite was professional wrestling with her hero Dusty Rhodes and his "Bionic Elbow". However, her favorite of all time had to be the Jerry Lewis Telethon. She religiously watched as much of the 24 - hour telecast as she could stay awake for and insisted on contributing herself each year personally delivering the money to the local TV station broadcasting the Telethon. Again, her concept of time and day was remarkable. She knew exactly the hour and day each was shown and rarely missed her TV favorites. In addition to her uncanny awareness of the day of the week and time of day, she had an established methodology of keeping track of annual events such as Christmas, her birthday, the Jerry Lewis Telethon, and other notable dates. She religiously kept a calendar with these on it and each year would copy the dates on to the next year's calendar. Truly remarkable for an individual with her IQ.

Sometimes her TV watching routines would result in unintended occasions of humor for the family. Once, when Dad Bradley was watching a football game, Kathy came into the room and expected to watch one of her favorite shows. It should be noted that, in addition to her must watch programs, she apparently felt she had to watch them on a specific TV - not that there was any shortage of TV's in the home since there were at least four. Since Dad Bradley was watching the game on the TV she simply had to watch her program on she tried to change the channel. He would not let her and she, in an extremely exasperated voice, indicated that she had "already seen this one." This became, and remains so today, a common statement among the family when there is a conflict over what program to watch.

While Kathy's language skills were limited to a somewhat significant degree, the family, having grown up with her, developed ways to interpret her speech rather effectively. As an example, Kathy loved Burger King Whoppers, French Fries, and a Coke. How she would request this dinner was by the specific request " –Bugger King hambugger, hinch fries, and coke." Some of her brothers and her sister believe that she limited her own speech abilities in our presence as a form of our own language between siblings. As an example, after Dad Bradley passed away and the siblings had all moved out of the house we would call the house to talk to Mom and if she was running errands Kathy would answer the phone. Clear as day Kathy would say" Dr. Bradley's residence!" Once the siblings spoke and she recognized our voice she would revert back to the familiar "family language". Friends of the family who called the house reported that Kathy would answer the phone with the same "Dr. Bradley's residence". When they asked for Mom Bradley Kathy would tell them she wasn't home. They would then ask Kathy to tell her that they had called and Kathy would respond that she would. Now, whether Kathy told her or not is debatable. There is rather humorous speculation among the siblings concerning the conversations she might have had with telemarketers calling the house when Mom was away running errands.

Her functional use of language and an awareness of situations was demonstrated once when she "saved" her younger brother Chris. She was eight years old and Chris was five. Until more houses were built in our neighborhood on the Caloosahatchee River, there was a horse pasture next to our property. One day Chris had wandered into the pasture and was in apparent danger from the horses. Kathy recognized the situation as something not right, went into the house, and somehow communicated to Mom that Chris was in danger. Mom came and retrieved Chris from the horse pasture and disaster was averted. Again, it is interesting that she was able to discern the danger and communicate that to an adult given her IQ level and age.

Over the years LARC and Lee County provided many recreational and sporting activities in which Kathy participated. There were regular dances and Kathy rarely missed any of these. She was an enthusiastic dancer and treated it as another outlet for her athletic abilities. Her particular expertise, and for which she became somewhat famous locally, were the Macarena (taught to her by Dick's wife Di who worked at LARC) and the Belly Dance (for which she had formal lessons). She would exuberantly "dance like nobody was watching". One morning Mom called my wife Di to the front window. Kathy was waiting for the bus by the roadside in front of the house to take her to work. She always had music with a headset. She was dancing like Michael Jackson Di tells me - just like nobody was watching!

She had a regular boyfriend for more than 30 years to whom she was very loyal. They had a very close relationship since he was allowed to "kiss my ring" (literal, not a euphemism) - that act being the epitome of love as far as she was concerned.

Her knowledge of human sexuality and relationships was another product of her sister - in - law Di. In her role at LARC, Di was responsible for classes in Human Growth and Development. One of the more notable things she learned was that she was a "grown woman" - this concept originally meant to discourage any childish displays of temper when things did not go her way. Thereafter, and much to the dismay of her Mom and others, she used this relentlessly as an argument in support of many things she wanted to do, or did not want to do as the case might be, always couching her arguments cleverly as she was a "grown woman." When Kathy was 26 years old she was given a hysterectomy. This was a decision by Mom and Dad based upon their fear that someone would try and take advantage of her intellectual disability and lack of understanding about sexual issues.

Special Olympics became an important part of Kathy's life. After the first games in 1968 this organization, founded by Eunice Kennedy Shriver, spread quickly and came to Ft. Myers early on. Kathy became an early, relentless and very successful participant - frequently cheered on by her brothers and later by her sister. Beginning at about age 14 she participated until shortly before her death at age 60. There are not many Special Olympics sports in which she did not participate. The first sports available were track and field so she ran, jumped, threw softballs and did anything else that was offered. As an adult, she also participated in Special Olympics bowling, golf, bocce ball, and basketball. However, over the years swimming was clearly her forte. She swam every stroke - freestyle, backstroke, breast, and even butterfly. She had been from an early age, and would continue to be throughout her entire life, part fish! Her last sport covered the final five years of her life and she pursued it with the same relentless determination she had every other. The Equestrian and horsemanship competitions became her last passion and, as with every other sport she tried, she excelled. Perhaps her ultimate accomplishment in Special Olympics was her participation in the 1992 International Special Olympics Summer Games in Barcelona, Spain.

Her prowess in Special Olympics is partially demonstrated by the hundreds of ribbons displayed on her multiple bulletin boards. Her Barcelona Olympics badge is displayed in the upper right corner of the large board. Following her death her siblings counted the ribbons and medals on these two boards and found about 300. There were many hundreds more in boxes in her room. A truly dedicated and talented athlete!

In all things sports and physical Kathy was nothing if not extremely competitive - perhaps a result of growing up and living with five brothers and a sister who were all into a variety of sports. A good example of this was the experience of older brother Jim's wife Suzanne. She had volunteered to officiate/assist at a local Special Olympics event in the early 1980s. For her service she received a small trophy in appreciation. Kathy had earned a 1st place blue ribbon in some event...and insisted on trading her blue ribbon for Suzanne's trophy apparently believing it signified a greater degree of success than a ribbon.

The only sport her siblings can recall she failed to master was water skiing. Since the family lived on the Caloosahatchee River in Ft. Myers, they naturally gravitated to sailing, water skiing, and fishing. Over the years there were all manner of boats lined up on the seawall and dock in front of the family home including, of course, a ski boat. Her siblings tried to teach Kathy to water ski to no avail. She did not seem to grasp the "stand up" part. Consequently, when the power was applied she would essentially plow through the water to the point of near drowning - all the time with a giant grin on her face! But because she would never give up on anything, she would not let go of the tow rope for any reason. Her siblings would stop the boat, tell her to stand up, and repeat the process. Although she never mastered it we believe she enjoyed it immensely.

Kathy also had some rudimentary awareness of social welfare issues as well. When Dad got sick in 1985 she became a frequent and dedicated blood donor. Later in life she loved wearing her "10 Gallon Donor" tee shirt. She also knitted in her free time. She would make squares which Mom Bradley would sew together into Afghans and other items. Kathy then delighted in going to the county nursing home, Shady Rest, and giving them to the elderly people living there. She did this for decades. She also was in Girl Scouts and earned a number of merit badges, particularly in the area of helping others.

Kathy also had a spiritual life. Her Catholic Church in Ft. Myers had a special program for people with intellectual disabilities and she received her First Communion at about age 15. She attended church regularly for many years. In her final 8 years or so she attended a Baptist church with her group home housemates which allowed her to play her harmonica to the hymns along with the choir.

One would not want to leave the impression that all was perfect in our world with Kathy. There were many challenges - mostly related to her being rather stubborn (a trait she shares with several of her siblings). While not universal, it is accurate to say that many individuals with Down Syndrome tend to be ritualistic and frequently develop elaborate patterns of behavior to achieve some tasks. Kathy was no different and she would react strongly if one tried to get her to cut any tasks short. She voiced her unhappiness with a loud, "Not my way!" Peace would only be restored when she was allowed to complete whatever ritual she was engaged in.

A couple examples should suffice to illustrate. When all the other siblings had begun their careers or gone off to college, my wife Di and I used to stay at the Bradley house with Kathy when they traveled to medical conventions and other destinations. Once I noticed Kathy was doing a very poor job of brushing her teeth and felt like I needed to improve her technique and the results. After some verbal prompting and demonstration failed to produce what I considered adequate results, I attempted some hand over hand assistance. As indicated earlier, Kathy was very athletic and quite strong. This turned into a significant physical struggle and was accompanied by screaming and yelling that could be heard around the neighborhood. Big mistake - nothing good came as a result. Sometimes it was just better to leave well enough alone. Additionally, later I learned that brushing was painful for Kathy as she had tooth and gum disease.

On another occasion there was a dance scheduled of which Di and I had no prior knowledge. One of us would have had to take her into town, about 5 miles. By the time we realized this event was planned and Kathy *always* attended previous obligations would prevent either of us from taking her to the dance. I tried to no avail to explain this to Kathy but she always went to these dances and she was going to go come hell or high water. The house was very large and rambling. It got eerily quiet and we discovered she was gone. In order to get to this dance she had to walk a two lane, 55 mile an hour, unlighted road with no sidewalks or shoulder for two miles to busy U.S. 41. It was then about 3 more miles into town to the dance.

Once we realized she had left the house we were frantic as to her whereabouts. We called the sheriff's department for help in locating her. The Bradley home was immediately outside the Ft. Myers City Limits so this was the correct call. However, the sheriff's call center insisted that it was a Ft. Myers Police issue so, in desperation, I called there. They, of course, said it was a sheriff's department responsibility. Having notified both agencies and asking them to put a call out to all their patrol cars to keep an eye out regardless of whose responsibility it was, we began to search ourselves. It never occurred to us that she would try to walk to the dance. We did not believe she knew much about how to get around, it was night and it was quite distant. Di, however, in driving around looking for her decided to go by the dance venue. Incredibly, she saw Kathy walking determinedly along U.S. 41 about 3 blocks from the venue. She stopped and said, "Get in the car." Kathy cheerily said, "Oh, hi Diane" and immediately got in. We never really understood how stubborn and determined she could be until this incident. I never doubted it again.

Incidentally, it was mentioned earlier that part of her daily work week routine each evening was to make her lunch for the next day. This is a skill that can be attributed to Di. On another occasion our parents were gone the notes Mom left included making Kathy's lunch for work. Di simply decided Kathy was perfectly capable of making her own lunch and proceeded to help her do so for a couple days. From then on Kathy did it religiously on her own each evening before a work day. Di reminded us all that the expectations we have for people with I/DD have real world results. When we assume they can't, they can't. When we assume they can with guidance, typically they can and will become more independent individuals.

An example of Kathy's more raw side was an occasion when her sister Carolyn and her boyfriend Jim (now husband) visited the Bradley home from Orlando where they were attending the University of Central Florida. Unfortunately the home was laid out such that Jim was assigned to Kathy's bathroom. Since all the siblings had by now left the home, Kathy was not used to sharing it with anyone. As this was not Jim's first visit, Kathy knew him pretty well. She also knew when he visited she would be required to share her bathroom with him. When Jim came into the house with his luggage Kathy's immediate, exasperated and very put upon response was, "Oh no, not *you* again!"

Another example of her need for structure and stubbornness was in her determination to maintain her set routine and complete everything as she always did. She was swimming her specified number of laps in the pool one day when thunder and lightning began to come closer to the house. Mom, Di, and I were sitting on the pool deck talking when this began. Mom told Kathy to finish her current lap and get out of the water because of the lightening. Kathy kept swimming since she had not transferred all the pennies to the "completed laps" end of the pool. Mom told her again - she kept swimming. Again with the same result. Then Mom jumped in the pool completely dressed and pulled her out of the pool. Mom was about 75 years old when this happened. Kathy's need for routine was absolute - again, not unlike many people with Down syndrome. Di and I still chuckle about this incident today.

As a direct result of Kathy's influence in the family, her brother Roger earned a degree in Special Education from Florida State University and began a career in the public schools and a short stint at the Sunland Training Center in Ft. Myers. When an opening as the Executive Director of The Arc of Lee County occurred, he applied. He became the Director of this community based organization, which Kathy attended from age five until her death, for 31 years from 1986 until his retirement in 2017. Roger became well known in the I/DD community throughout Florida and served on many committees and other interest groups. He was an exceptionally passionate, calm advocate with community organizations, the County Commission, and state government agencies.

The second oldest in the family is me. I similarly carved out a career in services and supports to people with I/DD. I also graduated from FSU with a degree in Education and later a Master's degree in administration. My work in the field covered a total of 41 years. I began as a direct care worker at the Sunland

Center in Ft. Myers and eleven years later became the Superintendent. The last 18 years of my career was as the CEO of The Arc chapter in Gainesville, Florida which provided services and supports to about 400 people in that community. Like Roger, I became well known (perhaps notorious is a better description) throughout Florida and nationally as a consultant and expert in civil litigation. I served on the Board of Directors of The Arc of Florida for many years, ultimately becoming its President. I was the third family member to serve on the Board of Directors of The Arc of Lee County. I did so for about five years until my brother Roger was selected as the CEO at which time I resigned as I felt that would be a clear conflict of interest. I also have served for many years on the Florida Developmental Disabilities Council, a federally funded organization influencing public policy and funding for developmental disabilities, as an appointee of the Governor.

Brother Brian became an architect. The title of Brian's Master of Architecture thesis was "Residential Facilities for the Developmentally Disabled." Over the years he has provided many, many hours of pro bono professional services to The Arc in Lee County. His work included architectural plans, designs and construction management for building construction and renovations. These efforts included the buildings at the main facility as well as the group homes. He is currently planning the design of a Culinary Program kitchen addition to one of the buildings. Brian currently is the fourth member of the family to serve on The Arc of Lee County's Board of Directors over the last 67 years.

Other siblings are involved as well. Chris and Carolyn are regular donors to The Arc in Lee County. Chris organizes the annual donations of the siblings to The Arc of Lee County. It is accurate to say that all of Kathy's siblings are very strong advocates for people with I/DD. Chris believes that Kathy is the primary reason he has no tolerance for bullies.

None of us ever let a disparaging comment about our fellow human beings with disabilities go unchallenged. All of us love to tell stories about Kathy and what she is capable of. We all believe that people with intellectual and developmental disabilities are fundamentally so much more like us than they are different from us.

Younger siblings Chris, Brian, and Carolyn all remember what they did when their friends would first come to the family home. They all report that they would not warn first time visitors they had a 'retarded' (term used at the time) sister. They simply introduced her to these people and them to her. Kathy would respond, "Oh, hi John." They all believe that these normal introductions and interactions resulted in a number of people who had perhaps never encountered a severely disabled person before perceiving such individuals in a positive way - hopefully for the rest of their lives.

Advocacy and support for people with intellectual disabilities has also been passed down generationally from Kathy's siblings. Di's and my daughter Brooke became a Registered Nurse and practices strictly in Neonatal Intensive Care (NICU). Babies born with severe disabilities frequently spend considerable time in these specialized medical care units. Brooke was always close with Kathy and enjoyed her immensely which created a special place in her heart for disabled children.

Brother Roger and wife Deryl's (Special Education teacher) daughter Meghan earned a Ph.D. in physical therapy and provides services in the Early Steps program for children with I/DD. Their son Matthew is an engineer with Exxon Mobile in Houston and chairs the United Way work day and ensures that it is always related to people with special needs. Youngest son Michael did his Eagle Scout project at The Arc in Ft. Myers. I mentioned earlier that Kathy loved music and she also loved to dance. In High School when Michael was at Mom's house, Kathy would frequently ask him to slow dance with her in her room. He would always happily do so and Kathy was in heaven dancing with her head on his chest. He earned a Master's Degree in Landscape Architecture and worked a large project in Miami providing ADA compliant access and exercise equipment for a walking park. He was one of the first on site at The Arc in Ft. Myers after devastating Hurricanes Charlie in 2004, Irma in 2017 and most recently Ian in 2022.

Brother Chris looks back and reflects on the effect that Kathy's presence potentially had on the neighborhood kids - that while different than the rest of us she was perceived as another neighborhood kid - and how they perceived people who were different than themselves later in their lives, which we cannot know for certain. However, he recalls one specific person who grew up in Ft. Myers with Kathy's older brothers. His name is Ross Webb. He became a local pharmacist and has served on the Board of Directors at the Lee County Arc for over 30 years even though his only connection with individuals with I/DD had been the Bradley family. Mr. Webb has been exposed to and aiding, through LARC, for decades all the families in the Ft. Myers area with children with I/DD who sought to include their children in the community rather than isolate them from society. Including Kathy in all family activities exposed people in the Ft. Myers community to people with I/DD before mainstreaming became the "enlightened" way of dealing with those with I D/D popular in the late 1970s.

Clearly, Kathy's birth, early development, and place in the family had a profound effect on her siblings. Roger and I especially would come to believe that Kathy brought focus and direction to our lives and have been keenly grateful to her. Just as certainly, the decision to keep Kathy at home with family had a truly profound effect on her, her development, her other siblings, and their children as well. As a result of her staying with the family, she became quite independent; she progressed far, far beyond the expectations communicated to the family when she was born; she became an active participant in her community; and she led a fulfilling life as a productive worker who paid taxes.

When Kathy died, several of her siblings gathered around Mom Bradley (Mom was 96 at the time) at her house and brother Roger told Mom Kathy had died. She started to weep a little and then noted that her brothers and sister had all treated her so well. Roger responded with "We just watched you and Dad and followed your example." It is hard to believe Roger found those words in that moment; it was truly profound. The siblings thought about what Roger said and thought about the "family culture" that was established and the need to preserve it. We believe we have successfully done precisely that.

To provide additional context for Kathy's life, the family patriarch, Dr. James L. Bradley, passed away on February 1, 1985 at the age of 66 when Kathy was 31 years old. This left Mom Bradley, at the age of 65, the remaining caregiver and legal guardian for Kathy. Although, by this time Kathy was quite independent even though still living at home. Mom Bradley, while still serving as Kathy's caregiver thought it prudent to make Roger and me her legal guardians. At the age of 88 Mom had a Transient Ischemic Attack (TIA) or mini stroke and as a result was thereafter unable to drive. While we cannot know her thoughts at the time we can speculate that she saw this limitation on her part as a potential threat to Kathy's safety if something happened to her or to Kathy. It was a short time later that Mom decided to move Kathy into a Group Home for people with ID/D where she lived for the next 8 years until her passing. For those 8 years she continued to work at the Lee County Arc and live an active life by participating in events arranged by the Group Home such as church, horseback riding, bowling, dances, and much more. It is instructive to note that Kathy, with her two housemates, was as supportive to them as her family had been to her. Kathy would "mother 'the two of them since they were not as capable as she was.

Visiting Kathy at the Group home or having her come to Mom's for holiday get - togethers did present a challenge in the first year, or so. If Mom Bradley went to visit Kathy in the Group Home she seemed to have the impression that Mom was coming to take her back "home". The same can be said about the holiday get - togethers – Kathy seemed to think she would be staying at mom's home after the get - together ended and moving back in.

Kathy passed away January 17, 2016 at the age of 60. At the time of her birth in 1955 the life expectancy of people born with Down Syndrome was about 25. Although there are frequently heart issues such as murmurs associated with Down, many researchers believe this early mortality was strongly correlated to the fact that most were institutionalized and were exposed to many nosocomial (originating in the facility) infections. Eddie Burke died at the age of 57 and Kathy Bradley aged 60. They both died in a similar fashion. They were very healthy until a very short, complete crash of mental and physical functioning. This is not at all unusual for people with Down Syndrome. It is my belief that both died from the complications of what I have come to call "extremely rapid onset Alzheimer's Disease."

One of the main characteristics of Alzheimer's disease is the presence of large accumulations of Beta Amyloid Plaques in the brain. There is a gene on chromosome 21 which produces a protein called amyloid precursor (APP). Too much of the amyloid precursor causes buildups of these Beta Amyloid Plaques. Since most people have two chromosome 21 sets a normal amount of APP is usually produced. However, individuals with Down Syndrome have three Chromosome 21 sets and, consequently, more APP than normal is produced which apparently results in more Beta Amyloid Plaques. By age 40 almost 100% of people with Down syndrome have at least some of these plaques in their brain. That does not mean they have Alzheimer's at this point but they are almost all well on the way to developing it.

In addition to my sister, I have known several other persons with Down Syndrome that died in a similar manner. Eddie Burke apparently experienced a similar phenomenon. It is my belief that this bears further investigation.

In any event, as a direct result of the family decision to have Kathy remain at home with her parents and siblings despite all the advice received to the contrary, she lived an exceptionally healthy, full, productive, loving, and successful life. In turn, she made her family's life much more full as well.

Her family has always, and continues to, thank God for her being part of their lives. An exceptionally special person who brought joy, insight, and purpose to her family. In many ways she is the best among us.

PART THREE

Anderson Burke

Eddie Burke

Eddie and I have worked out a routine for my visits: I arrive at The Arc around 2:00 PM. We greet each other with a bastardized version of American Sign Language's sign for "brother." Kathy had mentioned Eddie had been exposed to ASL so I learned the correct sign from a friend Angie Wade. The first time I greeted Eddie with the sign, he immediately repeated it, shaking his head vigorously and verbalizing. Over time, Eddie and I corrupted the sign down to a quick crossing of our hands at the wrists with our thumb and forefinger forming an "L." When I greet Eddie now, I make the Burke sign of brothers. He does the same, rocking his head to and fro rapidly and laughing.

Once the greeting is completed, Eddie grabs my hand and leads me straight to the car. There is no time to stop at the front desk and check him out. He is ready to go. I hold the door open for him and once in the seat, I hand him the seatbelt buckle. He always takes a moment to tuck in the front of his shirt before fastening the seatbelt. We stop at a fast food chain and order hamburger, fries and two Cokes. The fries he eats immediately. His Coke is drained. He places the empty Coke cup on the floor between his feet and emits an enormous belch then a loud vocalization as the first rush of caffeine hits. If I am quick I can get a sip or two of my own drink. Eddie glances my way. My Coke becomes his Coke. It disappears in two or three sips. Often, Eddie pounds the back of his head with an open palm to defeat a brain freeze. He saves the hamburger for later.

As he is eating and drinking, Eddie gestures at upcoming streets I need to turn. The first time he did this, I ignored him and became lost. Now I follow his lead. He is cross - eyed and nearly blind but knows where I should turn. When convinced I am on the correct road, he relaxes and stares at his hand, turning it over and over as a botanist would examining a newly discovered flower.

If we are in my wife's car Eddie will open the hatchback and search through Julie's stash of 3M stickers she keeps for handing out at trade shows. She always adds more stickers to the stash prior to visits with Eddie. One of the stickers exclaims, "Women Working." This is one of Eddie's favorites and a handful will be poached.

The Williams - Young House is located on the corner of a quiet leafy neighborhood street and a noisy four lane county road about 15 minutes from The Arc. At the House, we plow through the front doors holding hands and march back to Eddie's room saying quick hellos to residents and staff.

The House's eight residential rooms are bisected by a large industrial kitchen, a dining area, living room with a TV and a small administrative office.

Eddie's room is 10'X 12'. He has a chest of drawers, a single bed, a closet, a desk and chair. A 19" TV, purchased by Betty and kept at high volume, sits atop the chest of drawers. Eddie keeps the TV tuned to the Eternal World Television Network, a channel devoted to Catholic Church teachings and becomes upset if the channel is changed. Adorning the walls are numerous photos, stickers, articles and framed photos he has attached with tape, thumbtacks or nails. The walls are littered with tiny holes. These Eddie helps repair during the maintenance man's regular visits to his room.

Once in his room, Eddie places the now cold hamburger on his desk and removes the buns. These are waded up in the paper and left on his desk to be tossed later. He picks up the meat patty and in a short time it is gone. Now it is time for work. For the next fifteen minutes, we are busy, pinning or stapling photographs of people or beautiful scenery to a bulletin board. Each photograph must be placed on the board as Eddie determines. If I pin one on a spot not to his liking or slightly off center, Eddie will shake his finger at it and point to an empty spot where the photo really belongs. Once placed in the correct area Eddie will clap his hands and utter, "gud, gud, gud, gud…"

Not all visits have gone well. Early in our relationship, I stopped in to see Eddie at his desk at The Arc. I must have caught him in a foul mood or startled him because as I leaned near him he head butted me with such force that I was momentarily stunned. The sound of the strike alerted a staff. She rushed over.

"Are you OK?" she asked. In truth I did not know where I was after the blow but responded with a weak thumbs up. It was all I could muster. After ten or fifteen seconds I recovered from the shock. Throughout that time, Eddie resumed working.

We have had only one other incident when Eddie scratched my face near my right eye as he tried to forcibly remove my glasses. I told him "NO!" sharply. To date, he has not grabbed at my glasses nor, thankfully, head butted me. I am more wary however when I lean in close to him. Just in case…

When Eddie or another client of The Arc exhibits behavior such as striking another person, an incident report is placed in his file. If frequent enough, a behaviorist will be called in to work with the individual.

"I have never seen him angry," Michelle Yawn, a manager said. "I did see him react in an interesting way one day when another individual was screaming and we could not quiet him. Eddie walked to the table and began banging his own head on the tabletop. For whatever reason, this worked to quiet the resident."

Kathy Jackson related an incident that she clearly admits was her fault. She had forgotten that clients, like us all, have routines. Once a day, Eddie goes to the receptionist's desk with a stack of papers. Barbara is to place paper clips around the papers in a certain way the two had long ago worked out. Kathy was standing at the desk and observed this behavior for the first time. She reached for the paperwork. Eddie began to pummel her. It shocked her.

"I should have stayed out of it. I will not do that again," she says.

Despite the rare misbehavior, Eddie's life is varied and meaningful around the House. His day begins early around 5:00 AM. He is able to dress himself in his standard jeans and a white t - shirt. When dressed, he sets the table and when eating sits at the head of the table observing the goings on of the House as residents are preparing for the day. When he returns from The Arc in the late afternoon, Eddie heads straight to the kitchen and helps prepare the table for dinner by laying out the plates and silverware.

Some Sundays find Eddie attending church with one of the staff.

"He is very scheduled driven," Jeanette Wilson says. She is a Program Coordinator and was also in charge of the Williams - Young House at one point. She has been with The Arc for many years. "He will sit at the dining table or in the living room and do his paperwork, always observing the residents. He is like a businessman, always going through papers, adding them or pulling them out of a notebook." The papers Jeanette refers to are stacks of plain 8x10 sheets of paper Eddie will perforate with a three - hole punch. He might draw on the sheets or staple photographs to them.

If work is required on the house, Eddie will follow the service person around observing their every move. One plumber, scurrying under the house to repair a leak heard something behind him and turning to see what the noise was, illuminated Eddie's dirt smudged face with his flashlight beam. If shelves need to be installed, Eddie is the person called on to do it. He has, as one staff person described, "an innate ability to understand how things go together." Missed spots on the wall have been pointed out to surprised painting contractors. He will walk through the parking lot checking to make sure each car door is locked. When the dinner plates are cleared, Eddie empties the House's trash before retiring to his room for more paperwork and TV before sleep.

Although at both The Arc and the Williams - Young House, Eddie is somewhat aloof, he has developed several relationships since his time with The Arc. According to Michelle, Eddie has a protective feel for those less fortunate than he.

"I would say the one defining characteristic of Eddie is his empathy, his understanding of other's emotions, his ability to understand someone is suffering or not feeling well. If someone has fallen, Eddie will try and help them up. If this doesn't work, he will go to the office and get a staff person. If Amy (a resident) is upset, he will rub her shoulders. This is unusual." To further illustrate her point, Michelle related the story of an individual in the House who had been hospitalized on numerous occasions. Each time he was carried out of the House on the gurney, Eddie was at his side showing concern for his well - being. Finally, the man was too ill to remain at the House and spent his last days with Hospice. At his death, the room was cleaned and repainted. Eddie collected all of the man's photographs and now keeps them stored in his room.

Michelle joined The Arc at age 19 after spending time with an aunt who was cared for by the organization. Starting as a direct care provider, she spent her off hours assisting the residents any way she could and pursued continuous training programs. Like many of the people I met associated with The Arc, Michelle could have a career in the business world away from the stress of caring for so many individuals with disabilities. Although quick to dismiss the idea, Michelle, has special empathy, a desire to care for those who cannot care for themselves. I saw this selflessness over and over in the people I met associated with The Arc and with previous encounters with Sunland staff. She, though, is not an idealist. She has seen too much in her eleven years at The Arc and has little patience for new hires who see individuals like Eddie as "

'God's little angels who need their care.' These people do not last long," she says. "I want to help the individual grow, to understand the dignity and experience of making mistakes. I have seen this growth in Eddie since I have known him. He can go further in his development.

"We have a twenty - one - year - old man, Ronnie, who is very small and suffers overwhelming medical related problems. When he first joined us, Eddie had an immediate attraction to him. He watched as Ronnie was brought into the House and checks on him whenever he can. Ronnie is basically bedridden, very fragile. Eddie understands Ronnie needs protection…he will hover over him and watch or stroke him. Eddie can be very loud with his vocalizations but when he is with Ronnie in his room, Eddie is very quiet, sensitive to Ronnie's feelings. I have not seen this behavior in Eddie before. This is a big thing. This is the growth I referred to earlier."

Eddie for his part is quite fond of Michelle. It is impossible to say what feelings he has for her but to offer an observation that he acts like an adolescent with a crush would not be a stretch. He sits by her as she does paperwork as long as he is quiet and will burst into staff meetings to hug or kiss her. For her part, Michelle speaks to Eddie as she would another adult. She does not use simple sentences or commands such as are given to the pet dog. She engages him in meaningful dialogue and although Eddie cannot speak he makes it clear that he understands what she is telling him. He wants to be a part of what is going on and staff such as Michelle recognize this and include him in almost every activity. When she is heading to the store, Eddie will hop in the car and help her with the shopping. If he wants something at the store he will gesture toward it.

"I like his spirit," Jeanette Wilson says. "He is the helper of the House. He loves to take care of any chores that need to be done. Decorating at holidays. Wherever there is a need, Eddie is there to help. He communicates so well without speaking and looks out for the smaller ones."

When asked what working with individuals like Eddie means to her, Jeanette said simply, "I feel like I am making a difference."

* * *

My involvement in Eddie's world gave me an appreciation of the selfless, often thankless work caretakers such as Michelle, Jeanette and Carolyn do. Each professional interviewed shared the common thread of caring for those who cannot care for themselves. In order to shine a light on this characteristic trait, I chose Kathy Jackson as a representative of the wonderful caretakers I met on this journey.

Kathy was raised in the small town of Perry, Florida, located fifteen miles from Apalachee Bay in the crook of Florida's Gulf coast. While she was working on a Masters degree at Florida State University in 1979, her husband was killed in an automobile accident. This abrupt hit sent her reeling back home to the safe embrace of family and friends.

"I had recently graduated from college with a degree in Social Work and had enrolled in the Master's program for Guidance and counseling. I had taken a couple of days off from school to help a friend scheduled for a C - section. I had planned to stay for a few days to help with her daughter Aaron. It was 11:00 in the evening and we were all preparing for a night of sleep before the big day arrived. Suddenly the phone rang; my father - in - law was calling to let me know that Brad had died in an automobile accident on the road outside of our apartment; our neighbor had identified him at the scene, that witness could have been me. I moved back to my hometown where I knew I could surround myself with people who would help me through this very difficult period of my life's journey. It had only been 3 months since his death, I was 24 years old, and I was still reeling from pain and uncertainty. I needed to find a place to recover.

"Brad had been my high school sweetheart. I was devastated," she says.

After three months of recovery, Kathy applied for and was offered a position of social worker with Taylor County Association of Retarded Citizens.

"For the first two weeks of employment I was completely lost. I began to question if this was the right job for me. I walked through the hallway quickly to avoid the client's morning greetings. I constantly asked myself, 'what is wrong?'

"Taylor Arc occupied one wing of the school that once housed the segregated high school for students of color. After reviewing my credentials and going through the question and answer phase of the interview, I accepted the job as the Social Worker for the Taylor Association for Retarded Citizens. Becky Maguire the Executive Director followed the offer of the job with a tour of the program. I then was introduced to the people earlier passed in the hallway who would turn out to be the first real teachers in my life.

"I had moved to Perry with my family when I was 3 years old. Being a small town, most people knew each other and their families. The people I was meeting at Taylor were unfamiliar to me. The interview provided a basic overview about the people The Arc served but through the introductions, I could only speculate what role I would play in their life's path. I knew this journey would take time. For the first 2 weeks of my employment, I was completely lost; I understood for the most part, what the paper work duties entailed but the bigger part of the picture was still missing for me. My anxiety quickly mounted and I began to question if this was the right job for me. I already had a heavy heart and I just did not need any additional burden. Each day I walked through the hallway and my pace quickened each day to avoid the clients' morning greetings. My intellectual self was questioning, 'what is wrong with you?'

"My desk was located in the administrative wing, which was actually just another classroom in the old school. There were four desks in the classroom, one desk was situated in the center of the room which faced south this desk was reserved for the Executive Director, Becky Maguire. The desk to the left in the room was reserved for Janet McCall The Arc's Bookkeeper/Executive Secretary/Counselor/and Everything Else person. My desk was to the right in the room and was the desk furthest from the door. It was the perfect triangle. I knew that Becky was the most important presence in the room and I adored her. She and Janet were the perfect people for this moment in my life as they both had a wonderful sense of humor and tried to make me feel at ease in my new job. Unfortunately, I had to be the one to make that happen. Each day a person by the name of Mitch would greet me in the hall in his wheelchair. It was on the third week that Mitch followed me through the hallway onto the corridor and into our office. Thank God he did. He was a beautiful young man with cerebral palsy who was bound to a wheel chair that he controlled with his feet and some limited hand assistance. He wheeled his chair into my corner of the office with an apple in his lap and a grin that went from ear to ear. He approached my desk and with all that he could muster from his arms and hands, he grabbed the apple and plunked it on my desk. While it was startling to me, the light bulb went on in my heart and my soul. I finally understood his method of communication and I got his message loud and clear. He wanted to be my friend. On that day, I knew that this would be my life's calling."

Twenty - six - years after Kathy's revelation, I sent an email to her requesting information about my brother.

"I received an email late on a Friday afternoon. I recognized the name Burke. Could it be someone from Eddie's family? I realized the message and the potential of it was so amazing. I was being invited to help put an old disrupted puzzle together after 45 years of separation. This was what I had hoped for throughout my career."

Kathy was determined to make my first meeting with Eddie successful:

"I knew that every emotional detail of the reunion between Eddie and Andy would need to be handled with care. I carefully created my next e - mail to Andy, which I thought would help with his first meeting and offered some specific suggestions.

"Dear Andy: It's now Friday and I didn't want to forget to send you the information that I had promised. I've talked to a couple of staff that he is close to and they are so excited about the news of your visit. I would like to start off by sharing with you a few things that might be helpful to your first visit; this is the hand holding stuff that you mentioned. Eddie is extremely bright but this may not be apparent in the beginning. Visually he has what is called a tongue thrust which is a common characteristic of his syndrome. Eddie is not at all shy; he's usually the first person at the door to greet any visitor and usually has something to share. He has a tendency, actually a frequent tendency to make a high pitched verbal noise to note his excitement. This can be startling to those who don't know him. He's always busy doing things; he's not the kind of person who can just sit down. He usually reaches out to others to try to get them involved in whatever he's doing. It will take time to get to know him and his idiosyncrasies but you can start with bringing him a drink, Coke is his favorite. He loves 3 ring binders and paper and he enjoys putting holes in the paper so they don't have to be prepunched. I can imagine that in your effort to find out about him you've read through a lot of clinical mumbo jumbo, please set that aside and get to know Eddie through our eyes and it will be a heart warming experience. Look forward to seeing you. Kathy P.S. He also likes plain white t - shirts size medium.

"On the morning of August 16, I woke earlier than usual, as I too was anxious about the meeting. Also a resident of Jacksonville Beach I wondered if Andy lived close by. I took my usual walk along the beach and thought about the details of the meeting as I watched the sunrise. I took off for the office and paid particular attention to the details of my directions that I had given to Andy. I had provided him with the approximate amount of time it would take to make the trip, because I drive it every working day.

"I had already prepared Mary Williamson, the Director of the Day Program, Deborah Mock her assistant and Janet Pratt who worked directly with Eddie and they were excited and prepared for the visit as well. At this point, I had tried to think about every detail to make this first meeting a positive experience. Now it was time to watch nature take its course.

"It was apparent to my intuitive self that Andy was in search of his own 'Oz.' His home was not complete until he found his brother Eddie. As for courage, intellect and heart, just as it was in "The Wizard of Oz", they were always there. All that he needed were the red slippers and I hoped that I had provided his right size. The yellow brick road was before him.

"When Andy entered through my office door, I knew that this was a pivotal moment in his life - a chance to make his family complete again."

In addition to guiding me, Kathy was managing a large staff, overseeing numerous resident houses and most important, constantly having to appeal to law makers in Tallahassee for funding.

"Eighty percent of my job as Executive Director consists of dealing with funding sources. It is difficult to convince lawmakers to fund our programs. I am focusing now on just maintaining basic services. I am faced with cutting staff and reducing services to those in our care. One definite roll of government should be caring for individuals born with disabilities."

Most of the staff I interacted with were longtime employees of The Arc.

"I want my staff to be caring," Kathy says. "I want to see that in their soul. We do not wear uniforms. We do not want to do anything to differentiate ourselves from the clients. One cannot provide instruction and guidance without a bond. The staff tends to have good parenting skills, even if that person is not a parent. They must have a lot of physical strength, be self - assured, have great communication skills, thrive on a need to respond, know how to create a homelike atmosphere and maintain a routine for clients. There is lots of celebrating here. It is never boring. I want my staff involved.

"I am a true believer in the axiom, 'as human beings, who we are is how we care for those who cannot care for themselves.'"

***

Months after our introduction, I stopped in to see Kathy. As always, she took her valuable time for me. I asked her about George, Eddie's friend at Sunland Marianna who was transferred with Eddie in 1992 to St. Augustine.

"George was the son of an influential person," she said. "The family did not want anything to do with him. No one visited him. I knew his mother slightly and when we were together, she would never ask me about him. Disconnection from a child is a most difficult decision." Kathy paused, clearly upset by the memory.

"George has since passed away. He never saw his family."

An estimated 25% of families with a relative at The Arc are active with visits and gifts. Another 25% will visit once a year and the remainder has no contact at all.

I tell Kathy about letters Betty had written to an administrator at Sunland Marianna in the early 1990s, describing her pain and guilt in giving up Eddie.

"I wish so much your mother had sent those letters to me. I would have done anything to reconnect the family. I would have wanted your mother to understand the beauty in Eddie Burke."

The power in this simple statement illuminated everything Kathy, the staff at The Arc and both Sunland facilities came to represent for me. Despite their objections to such labeling, these are special people.

* * *

After developing a close relationship with Eddie, did I sweep in and take him home with me? No. He did not need to be rescued.

His life was good. The staff and residents at the Williams - Young House and at The Arc are Eddie's family. I am the newcomer. The staff knows best how to care for him and see that his needs and opportunities for growth are met. At one point Eddie had been transferred to a smaller group house in St. Augustine but had been unhappy and bored with the change. He missed the staff, residents and his routines. He successfully communicated this unhappiness and was returned to the Williams - Young House. In being an active part of Eddie's life, I am welcomed by Eddie and his extended family of caregivers and fellow residents as a part of his world.

I have learned, among other things, Eddie likes his tube socks and t - shirts white; he taps his left hand at the base of the thumb when he wants to go for a ride in the car and he likes his donuts cut into small pieces and placed in a bowl of cold milk.

And just as Carolyn Mayo and Jeannette Wilson related, Eddie loves to decorate at holidays. I drove to the Williams - Young House one Saturday just before Christmas. Eddie was in the front yard installing strings of Christmas lights around the decorative shrubbery in front of the building.

Several weeks later Eddie looked at me and said "HabbieNuuuYeeeee." It was clear as a bell.

* * *

On a bright fall day, I drove across town and picked up my father at his home. The weather was cool enough to keep the windows open in the car. We headed south.

It was close to Eddie's 48th birthday, my 55th birthday and two months shy of my father's 80th birthday. Almost a half - century had passed since the three of us had been in the same darkened house.

During the forty - minute drive to St. Augustine, my father reveled me with reviews of books he was reading, a continuation of a discussion on how mathematics can explain nearly everything and of his desire to visit his hometown of Bushnell, Florida. His interesting commentary made the drive pass quickly.

"I cannot believe we are here already," he said as we exited Interstate I - 95.

"It is all based on math," I said.

For the first time my father and I were visiting Eddie together. What was happening that October day was how I wanted to end this narrative.

Ten minutes later we turned on Sunrise Boulevard then onto the half - moon driveway of the Williams - Young House where my father's youngest son - and my brother lived.

POSTSCRIPT

Anderson Burke

Sitting in front of me now is a well - worn composition book. The corners are dog - eared and creased; the covers stained with coffee cup rings, ink blotches from leaky pens, several stickers from sporting good companies and the date "June '11 - " is written on the white label. This marks the start date for this particular comp book to distinguish it from all previous generations of comp books. When I have filled all one hundred pages, I will add the concluding month/year to the front cover and place it with previous comp books stored in neat rows on a shelf. About a third of the way into the book is a small cluster of gold aspen leaves glued to a page. Several pages beyond the aspen leaves is a page titled "things to do B4 leaving:" followed by a list complied to have completed before we left our home in New Mexico and returned to Florida. Most involved shutting down the small adobe home, making sure it was ready for winter. However, scrawled sideways in large black letters, some of the words and phrases words underlined, is the following:

ventilator. long time. cat scan. 2 neurosurgeons. not improve. amount of blood. so much swelling. subdural. 30 minutes. on breathing machine. brain bleed. pretty bad. surgery. herniation. DNR.

Someone finding my comp book could deduce these notes written against the grain of the page documented scary information provided by a medical professional. They would be correct.

On a cold January morning I received a call from an emergency room physician working at a hospital in St. Augustine, Florida. I paraphrase:

"Mr. Burke, this is Dr. - - - - and I have Edward Burke as a patient. You are his legal guardian, correct?" I confirmed. "He has suffered some sort of trauma to his head - we do not know exactly what happened - and we have basically two options at this point." Her explanation included all of the terms and words illustrated above. She concluded: "A neurosurgeon who examined your brother said he could perform surgery but feels it would not produce a successful outcome. Your other option is to DNR (Do Not Resuscitate) your brother. If this is your decision, we would place him in a darkened room…" she trailed off before adding, "you need to give me your answer within 30 minutes. There is another neurosurgeon who can give us a second opinion but he is in surgery now and may be unavailable in time." I told her I would call her back.

I looked down at the page, trying to make some sense of what I had been told, something that boiled down to the following: *Surgery useless. DNR your brother.* I glanced up at the clock and made a note of the time but did not jot it down in my comp book. All I remember now is that the big hand was on the Roman numeral II.

The first call I made was to Julie who was out of state traveling on business. After my summary, she concluded (as I was doing) if nothing could be done for Eddie we should make the hard decision to order DNR. But we both wanted more information before making that awful decision. I called my father. He was out running errands. Mary, his wife, said she would track him down and have him call me as soon as he could. This was reassuring. My next call was to Kathy Jackson of The Arc. She was aware of Eddie's situation and calmly listened to my increasingly rushed and panicked questions. During my conversation with Kathy, my father called. I thanked Kathy.

My father listened to my rambling summation. His questions were the questions a physician asks in trying to ascertain as much information as possible before offering advice. My problem was trying to explain something like "subdural" a one - word note on my page, a word I understood (incorrectly) to involve a leaking of blood under the skin to a medical professional. As my father tried to piece together what the medical situation was, an incoming called popped up on my phone screen. It was from the hospital. I told my father I would call him back as soon as I could.

"Mr. Burke, this is Dr. - - - - . Have you made a decision? We need to have an answer soon."

"Not yet," I said. "I was just talking to my father, Eddie's father, a physician, trying to explain the situation." Did I hope that knowing Eddie's father was in the same profession would help her in treatment of my brother? Yes.

"Have him call me, if he wishes," she said. "But we are running out of time." We hung up.

I sat in the chair, the phone held loosely in my hand. Can I DNR my brother? I glanced at the clock and noted how much time had passed. Thirty minutes is really no time at all. I needed something more. Who else can I call?

Michelle Yawn.

Although she had been promoted and no longer sees Eddie day to day, I assumed Michelle would be at the hospital with him and would give me a straightforward account of what was going on. I dialed her number. She was strangely cool and collected when I launched into a rapid - fire series of questions. I do not remember much of our conversation but she did say very clearly she had seen cases like Eddie's where surgery had been successful. This created a new scenario and gave me pause to reconsider the direction I was heading. The phone beeped with another call. It was the hospital again. How much time had passed?

"Mr. Burke, I have not heard from your father. Is he calling me? We need to have an answer from you as guardian." Dr. - - - - stated.

"I will call you back," I said. I remembered a friend, himself a retired ER physician at the same hospital this doctor practiced, telling me about the acronym, "GOMER." Get Out of My Emergency Room. Is this what was happing? Was Dr. - - - - rushing me so she could get Eddie out of her emergency room? I dialed Julie again and told her about my conversation with Michelle. There was a crack in fabric and some light and clarity was pushing through.

Five minutes later there was another call.

"Mr. Burke, my name is Dr. G - - - - . I am a neurosurgeon. I am with your brother Eddie and am taking him into surgery." My notes on the comp book page under the name, Dr. G - - - - are: *take to surgery. evacuate the clot. lots of swelling. put removed piece of cranium in abdomen.* Dr. G - - - - concluded with, "I will contact you later."

Suddenly, the decision had been taken out of my hands. I did not have to decide whether to have an operation done or to DNR him. This was totally unexpected. "Thank you Dr. G - - - - . Good luck and thank you," I said.

I made follow up calls to Julie and my father. My father inquired with gentle probing medical questions about Eddie's trauma and treatment. Questions I could not answer beyond repeating what sketchy and slim notes I had made.

Late that afternoon, after Dr. G - - - - called me and in turn I passed around the good news that Eddie had survived the surgery, the bleeding had been stopped and he would fully recover in about 6 weeks. I sat alone in the house contemplating how close I had come to making a decision that would have OK'd the medical staff to roll an unconscious, gurney'd Eddie Burke into a darkened hospital room and death.

I called Michelle and with a shaky voice thanked her for her subtle guidance. "Do you realize how close I came today to DNR'ing Eddie?" I asked. It was a stupid question. She was at the hospital with Eddie, listening and watching the events unfold. It my guess Michelle sought out Dr. G - - - - and convinced him to take Eddie into surgery. It is also my guess Michelle would never admit to doing so. I thanked her for caring for Eddie. I later found out at least three other employees of The Arc, including some who had retired from The Arc yet had rushed to the hospital when they heard of his condition.

***

On my first visit to see Eddie after he had been released and was well on the road to recovery, Donna Bougades, the Williams - Young House group home manager, told me about the day in the hospital waiting for my direction. "We were all crying, tears rolling down our faces. Just look at him now," she said. Eddie rose from his chair at the head of the table and was coming to greet me. The right side of his head had a massive half - moon shaped pink scar. Hair would soon cover the incision. Eddie grabbed my hand and led me toward the front door of the House.

"We will be back soon," I told Donna.

Eddie pushed opened the door and led me to my truck. "Do you want a Coke?" I asked him.

"Ya ya ya ya."

"Lets go then."

At the McDonald's drive - thru, a young woman leaned out of the pick up window holding a large Coke and straw. She looked into the cab of the truck and exclaimed, "Eddie!" Eddie squinted at the woman.

"Oh I used to work with Eddie. He is wonderful," she said.

"Thank you."

"Bye Eddie," she said as I pulled away.

"Bu bu bu bu bu bu...," he replied, waving goodbye.

***

Eddie passed away on July 5, 2017. He was 57 years old and in dying was surrounded by some of the Williams - Young House and The Arc staff who loved him. His death certificate listed no specific cause of death but to have lived for 57 years was an accomplishment considering a few decades prior those with Down syndrome rarely made it past their thirties.

A little over two months later I received a box sent USPS at our new home in Bend, Oregon. The young postal worker solemnly delivered the cardboard box marked 'HUMAN REMAINS' to our front door. She expressed sympathy at our loss. Hers was a nice courtesy. A few days later Julie and I drove Eddie's ashes to a small one - lane bridge 14 miles from our home. The bridge crosses Tumalo Creek, a clear fast flowing mountain stream strewn with beautiful orange and dark green rocks.

Eddie's grey ashes fanned out north and east in the strong current. We climbed up the bank then standing on the bridge mesmerized as the remains of my brother tumbled and floated away. Soon all that remained was a slight streak of heavier material settled on the bottom of the creek. These would take their time reaching the Deschutes River then the mighty Columbia River and finally the Pacific Ocean.

History and Future of The Arc

21 Dec '22
Alan Abramowitz
Chief Executive Officer
The Arc of Florida

The Arc of the United States is the largest national community - based organization advocating for and with people with intellectual and developmental disabilities and their families. As of 2023, The Arc of the United States has nearly 600 chapters in 47 states and has led the fight so individuals could live and reach their potential in their community for over eighty years.

The State of Florida has a long and successful history in advocating for persons with disabilities. Through tireless parent groups and legislation, The Arc of Florida has helped to open local chapters and community programs, called for institutions to close, and lobbied for change.

Timeline of important events in the history of what has become The Arc of Florida's legacy:

1915 Commission established to evaluate the need for an institution for persons who were "indigent, epileptic, and feebleminded."

1921 The Florida Farm Colony for the Feeble Minded and Epileptic opened in Gainesville. This was the beginning of State funded services for persons with developmental disabilities.

1950 The first convention of the "National Association of Parents and Friends of Mentally Retarded Children" was held. This group would later become known as The National Association for Retarded Children.

1953 The Florida Council for Retarded Children formed in Tampa by determined parents and friends with J. Clifford McDonald as the first President.

1954 Creation of Lee County ARC (LARC) with the establishment of the Riverside School by parents' response to the school system not serving students with an IQ below 50.

1957 The Florida Council for Retarded Children became affiliated with the National Association for Retarded Children.

1964 The Florida Council changed its name to Florida Association for Retarded Children (FARC).

1975 Community programs established as day training programs and community residential treatment programs. The Florida ARC worked with legislature to pass "A Bill of Rights for the Retarded."

1977 Six state institutions in Florida and one intuitional program for defendants in criminal justice system. Legislation passed for Florida Statute 393 which set the stage on how services would be offered in Florida.

1986 The Florida ARC chapter officially changed its name to ARC/Florida. Legislation passed to permit groups of six or fewer individuals to live in single family residential zones.

1988 ARC/Florida worked to have legislation passed that prohibited the use of noxious and painful stimuli in training programs as well expansion of the "Bill of Rights." Community services to the list of services authorized in statue

1993 ARC/Florida successful in working with family groups to pass legislation to establish Family Care Councils around the State.

1994 ARC/Florida successfully sponsored and had landmark legislation passed which prohibited the execution of individuals with mental retardation

2010 Official name of the corporation changed to The Arc of Florida

2012 The Arc of Florida received a special appropriation and began a dental treatment program that has successfully served individuals in their community for the last ten years.

2013 The Arc of Florida initiated legislation to "End the R Word" in Florida, sponsored by Senator Thad Altman and Representative Janet Adkins and was signed into law by Governor Rick Scott.

2014 The Arc of Florida lobbied for the Stephen Beck, Jr., Achieving a Better Life Experience (ABLE) Act and was recognized on the floor of the Legislature for leadership on this issue.

The Arc of Florida continues to fulfill its mission today advocating for people with intellectual and developmental disabilities. There are currently 45 chapters and colleagues from Pensacola to Tampa to Miami. In addition, we have created a forum for small and moderate providers to speak with one voice as well as a monthly advocacy meeting for families and self - advocates as we maintain our commitment to grassroots advocacy. In the last several years, we have helped to eliminate the use of physical restraints at school, increased the budget significantly so Direct Support Professionals will make a minimum of $15 per hour, pushed for legislation to require parents to be informed of Agency Persons for Disabilities services for their school age children, as well as impacting community resources to support individuals living in their own community.

The Future of The Arc of Florida

Our priority in the future is to ensure the budget for services continues to grow with the increase of the cost of living and inflation. A top concern is to have the budget included in the Social Services Estimating Conference (SSEC). This is a consensus estimating conferences established with a responsibility of developing official forecasts of Medicaid caseloads and expenditures and state agencies are required to use these forecasts for planning and budgeting purposes.

Another urgent goal is to reduce the The Agency for Persons with Disabilities '(APD) Waiting List for those individuals eligible for Home and Community - based Waiver Program. Even though applicants are typically placed on a Waiting List when they are determined eligible, having an accurate picture of the numbers, names and locations of people who need services is essential if Florida is to develop more resources and state funds. The Arc of Florida and many local advocacy agencies use this data to educate our legislators about the unmet need in our State.

We will continue to promote and protect people with intellectual and developmental disabilities while actively supporting their full inclusion and participation in their individual community. Our advocacy involves self - advocates, families and providers sharing personal experiences and ensuring policy makers hear and understand what is needed for people with disabilities. The Arc of the United States and The Arc of Florida are and will continue to be a megaphone for this message.

Acknowledgments

There are so many people who are in some way responsible for my portion of this book about my sister Kathy. It would not have come to fruition without the help, encouragement, and input of numerous individuals who contributed in a variety of ways.

First and foremost, I want to acknowledge and recognize the importance of my sister Kathy Bradley. Despite her death seven years ago she inspires me even today. My life would not have been as full, productive, and joyful as it has been without her in it. She gave me purpose, direction, and a focus for all of my forty one year career in service to people with intellectual and developmental disabilities and beyond. For this and for her I am eternally grateful.

I especially thank my Mom and Dad for having the courage to keep Kathy at home with us when every authority and every piece of advice they received insisted that she be placed in the State institution as soon as possible.

Were it not for my friend and fellow author Andy Burke my portion of this book would never have been written. I so admire his determination to find and get to know his brother Eddie after a lifetime of not knowing him. My previous experience with family members in situations such as Andy's had always been that they had no interest in finding, nor making any effort to establish a relationship with, a family member who had 'disappeared" due to placement as a very young child in a state institution. It took a very special person to undertake this task and pursue it with diligence.

With regard to the material I gathered for the book, there are a number of family members I reached out to. Everyone enthusiastically responded with information, pictures, poignant antidotes, and funny stories of our life with Kathy. Contributing were my older brother Jim, younger brothers Chris and Brian, and my sister Carolyn. Since our brother Roger, who saw Kathy every weekday as the CEO of The Arc chapter in Ft. Myers where she worked, died in 2017, I could not access the wealth of information and experiences he had. However, his wife Deryl was very helpful in his stead. She was a Special Educator and was very involved with Kathy so she was an excellent resource as well.

However, as I have throughout my adult and professional life, I relied perhaps most of all on my wife of 44 years, Di. Since she was employed for a few years at The Arc chapter in Ft. Myers where Kathy was served and worked, she knew her well. She was also very close to Kathy in ways that I probably could not be since they are both independent, strong women. She not only encouraged me in the writing but also provided some excellent insights into Kathy and a number of the vignettes I have included. She is also an outstanding editor and suffered through many readings and re - readings of the manuscript. I could not have completed this task without her.

Dick Bradley
Oldsmar, Florida
January, 2023

***

Sometimes a person enters your life and before you know it you are off in a new direction. It can be a wonderful thing. In 2005 Kathy Jackson became for me an incredible force of discovery and wonderful change still reverberating today.

Special thanks to Neal Benson for his thoughtful review of the manuscript. Dina Justice of The Arc of Florida stepped up in the nick of time to design the book's cover and offer insightful editorial comments. Thank you Dina.

Sincere thanks to Alan Abramowitz for guiding this project to a successful conclusion. And to Dick Bradley for making Three Fields (A Brother. A Sister.) a more complete and touching story. You both are the solid foundations of this effort. Thank you.

And of course to Julie who loved Eddie and never once shied away from welcoming him into our lives.

Lastly I will never know what Eddie thought of my return to his world. Maybe I was simply a new face who provided him with car rides and fast food. But of course I hope he felt some fraternal connection to me as I did with him. Eddie was a good person and I loved him.

Anderson Burke
Bend, Oregon
January 2023

www.ingramcontent.com/pod-product-compliance
Ingram Content Group UK Ltd.
Pitfield, Milton Keynes, MK11 3LW, UK
UKHW062258290726
14090UKWH00017B/760

9 798987 870808